Intimations of Transcendence

Intimations of Transcendence

Autobiographical Essays in Context

Drew A. Hyland

RESOURCE *Publications* · Eugene, Oregon

INTIMATIONS OF TRANSCENDENCE
Autobiographical Essays in Context

Resource Publications
An Imprint of Wipf and Stock Publishers
199 W. 8th Ave., Suite 3
Eugene, OR 97401

www.wipfandstock.com

PAPERBACK ISBN: 979-8-3852-6036-2
HARDCOVER ISBN: 979-8-3852-6037-9
EBOOK ISBN: 979-8-3852-6038-6

VERSION NUMBER 10/23/25

Contents

Acknowledgements

As will become evident, I owe acknowledgement and thanks to so many people who have made possible the experiences about which I write in these pages; to my wife, Anne, to my sons, Chris and Craig, to my brother, Art, to my still growing extended family, to my teammates on the Princeton University Men's basketball team from many decades ago, to my former students, to my (most fortunately) too many to mention friends through the years. I hope the pages that follow give some inkling of my enormous debt to you all, for which I here offer heartfelt thanks. These thoughts simply could not have happened without you.

Introduction

THE WRITINGS THAT FOLLOW are not intended to conform to any standard format or genre of writing, and therefore the reader deserves an explanation of what is about to happen and why. This introduction will thus serve to introduce more the mode of presentation of the pieces that follow (and to an extent, their author) than the specific subject matters, which I hope will be self-explanatory.

My writing career as a professional philosopher, aside from occasional forays into 19th century philosophy, philosophy of art, and so-called continental philosophy, has concentrated in two areas: ancient Greek philosophy (my "field of specialization") and the philosophy of sport. Gradually, my work in these areas has come to focus on two themes, each of which has culminated in books in each domain. In Greek philosophy, concentrating on Plato, I have come to see the Platonic dialogues as exhibiting again and again a theme which I have tried to capture in the phrase "finite transcendence." To make a very long story short, Plato regularly portrays the human situation—and philosophy in particular—as an encounter with some sort of limitation or finitude (such things as the people one is with, a problem one must solve, something about which one is in *aporia*, or a limitation on one's own abilities) which one is called upon to transcend. One name Socrates uses for this group of situations is *aporia*, the *recognition* that we do not know, that we are somehow "at a loss" regarding a given topic or situation. At the same time, the dialogues teach us that we

1

must recognize an important ambivalence, that while some kind of transcendence of these limitations is possible and necessary, the actual transcendence available is almost always finite, itself limited by one dimension or other of our human condition. The ambivalence of the human situation is thus that we are constantly called upon to transcend, want to transcend, can transcend, but never in the complete or absolute way that, we usually think, would decisively solve our problems. In this sense, we humans are *always* "in aporia." It is the human condition. Hence the notion of "finite transcendence" as definitive of human aspiration.

In my work in the philosophy of sport, a central challenge has been the effort to understand what I have called the "stance" of play, the orientation or set of attitudes that we adopt when we play and how that stance differs from our ordinary or non-playful situations. Again to make a long and nuanced story short, I have characterized that stance as "responsive openness," a term meant to suggest that when we play, we at once are more open to possibilities presented to us, and more responsive to them, than we most often are in our non-playful stances. "Responsive openness" thus becomes on my understanding at once a description of the stance of play and an implicit recommendation of a way to be: more play-ful, that is, more open to our possibilities and more responsive to them.

Having developed independently in separate domains the notions of finite transcendence and responsive openness, it finally occurred to me that there is a deep kinship between them, and after the completion of one of my books (on Plato and the notion of finite transcendence) I wanted to develop more adequately that kinship, to join together what had too long been kept asunder. The question is, how to write such a work?

The Platonic dialogues and sport, as it turns out, share a number of characteristics, but one stands out immediately. The dialogues, by placing every philosophic discussion in a specific time and place, with specific characters and facing specific problems, are in this way the most concrete works of philosophy ever written. If the dialogue form tells us nothing else, it ought to tell us that Plato regarded the situation out of which any given philosophic discussion arises as of crucial importance both to the choice of topic and what is said about it. There can be no "abstract" philosophy for Plato, philosophy rooted in no time, no place, no specific human situation (although certain characters in the dialogues argue, usually unpersuasively, for such a position). The foundational question is and always is, how should we live? Philosophy, one might say in Plato's behalf, is among the most concrete of human activities. But so, surely, is sport, whose most notable characteristic is that it calls on us to join as one our mental and physical activities, our minds and bodies. Sport and the presentation of philosophy in the Platonic dialogues, we might say, are all about concreteness.

The last thing in the world I want to do, therefore, is to write a typically abstract academic treatise on these two themes whose most striking initial kinship is concreteness. I need to find a mode of presentation that might be true to its subjects, and that means a format that somehow embodies the concreteness of its subject matters. That clearly eliminates the now canonical format of academic philosophy, the treatise, which is virtually defined by its abstractness.

The first strategy that occurs to almost any student of the Platonic dialogues is obvious. Write a dialogue, in the spirit of the master. Everyone should try this; it deepens in a wonderful way one's appreciation of Plato's genius. Having discovered that one lacks the titanic genius necessary to write successful dialogues—that is, ones that are not merely concealed treatises—one must turn to other possibilities.

In what follows I have decided to try a format which, with some hesitation, I shall call autobiographical essays ("essay," after all, etymologically *means* "a try"). My hesitation is the fear of being misleading, which I shall attempt to counter right now. Although the essays that follow will look to many readers like autobiographies, they are not ultimately intended as such. Their point is not to inform the reader about *me*. Rather, I am *using* the format of autobiographical essays, exploiting that genre, in the service of a quite different end—hopefully as provocations to thoughtfulness, to philosophy. The appeal of an autobiographical framework should now be obvious; it, too, embodies that concreteness, that recognition that ideas and standpoints always arise out of specific contexts, present in the Platonic dialogues and definitive of sport. But I am no biographer or autobiographer. I might put the point this way; to understand the essays that follow simply as autobiographies would be like understanding the Platonic dialogues simply as dramatic plays. Something else is intended, something that I hope emerges in the work itself.

However, what emerges will not be "philosophy" in the technical, academic, and in my view too narrow sense. The pieces that follow are not full of arguments that prove this or that thesis, much less that refute anyone else's. One might with considerable, perhaps excessive generosity call them loosely "phenomenological," in that they attempt to reflectively clarify the structure and meaning of certain experiences. What I hope they are full of might be called—to borrow the wonderful phrase of the philosopher, Mitchell Miller, in reference to Plato—provocations, provocations to thoughtfulness and to philosophy. To put it one more way, my hope is to *evoke* matters for thought, to call them forth; I make no pretense to explain them, prove them, or refute their alternatives. They are intended to embody, then, the recognition of every artist, that there is more to life than can be contained in the propositional content of a sentence or even a treatise.

So I shall tell a number of stories about myself, about teaching, about playing basketball, about being married to an artist, about farming and fishing. But I shall try to use those personal experiences to elicit themes that are not merely about me (so limited, they would fail). Though I shall try to use the phrases as seldom as possible, all these experiences, I suggest in advance, embody the convergence of the themes of finite transcendence and responsive openness, perhaps as two streams, the Jeremy and the Black Ledge, originating in distant sources, converge as the Salmon River, which forms the southern boundary of the land on which I live. The essays that follow are some of the streams of my river.

Addendum

I began writing these autobiographical essays and completed drafts of them some twenty years ago, in the late 90's of the previous century and the early years of the present one. At the time, I did not seriously intend to submit them for publication—indeed, given the criteria for academic philosophical publication at the time, I doubted whether such publication would even be possible. And the single effort I made to interest a publisher in the volume confirmed my doubts at the time. Instead, I thought of them as what I occasionally referred to as "friends and family essays," occasional pieces that, perhaps one day, my grandchildren would enjoy reading. To say the least, much has changed since then, and there have been changes in what I would think about these issues and what I would want to say about them, as well as—happily in my judgment—a much more encompassing sense in the publishing world of what might count as philosophical thinking than was the case then. For those reasons, I have made two decisions: one, to venture to publish these essays for a larger potential audience, and second, to somehow and occasionally "update" the original essays. But how to do so? If I integrated the changes into the existing pieces written quite a while ago, I might no longer be true to what I was thinking then, at the time I first wrote the essays. On the other hand, if I made no changes or additions whatsoever, I would not, at least in some cases, be true to what I was thinking and experiencing now, how things have changed in the meantime.

So I have decided to do what I am doing even now in this addendum to the original introduction: I have left the original essays largely as I originally wrote them, and then, at the end of each essay, added an "addendum" as a set of reflections—some quite short, some longer—on how I might alter the essays now, or how I might just want to add to them. That way, at least I may hope that I have preserved what force there may be in my earlier reflections, and at the same time added something of what I might think now, at the ripe old age of 86. Somehow, I doubt if I'll need to do this again in another twenty years.

One more comment I'd like to add, then, about my earlier introduction. I spoke there of "concreteness" as an important marker of the kinship I found between the "finite transcendence" idea of my interpretation of Plato and the "responsive openness" that marked my understanding of the "stance" of play. To concreteness I would add, as a decisive kinship between the two themes, that of the question. As I have argued in so many of my writings, I find distinctive in the dialogues the primacy of the question in philosophy as the Platonic Socrates understands it. One might say that for the Platonic Socrates, the primary philosophic locution is not the assertion ("This is my philosophy . . .") but the question. The *aporia* that I found so basic to the Socratic philosophic stance leads essentially not to further assertions but to questions. To recognize that I am in *aporia* is to *question* that about which I am in *aporia*. That is why every Platonic dialogue begins (and ends) with questions: the question of courage, the question of justice, the question of friendship, or of love.

And I have come to recognize in my experience of sport the same primacy of the question, this time exhibited perhaps even more concretely. Every competitive game asks of each of the players each time they play, "Who can play the best today?" The common practice in playground games to choose sides "evenly" is done precisely to make the outcome questionable, to leave who will play the best—and win—an open question. I came to realize that a large part of both philosophy and competitive athletics for me is that in both spheres, I put myself in question. And, perhaps strange human being that I am, I love it!

CHAPTER 1

Being A Leaping Spark: Reflections on Teaching

"That which we are, we shall teach,
not voluntarily but involuntarily."

EMERSON, "THE OVER-SOUL."

MY FIRST SURPRISE ABOUT myself as a teacher came on the occasion of my first formal teaching experience. It was in the Fall of 1962, in my second year of graduate school. In my first year, as was customary at Penn State, where I earned my Ph.D, I had been the teaching assistant of a professor, sitting in on his lectures, grading the papers, and holding office hours. In this, my second year, I was given my own section to teach, an introductory course on logic. As I walked across campus to my first class, I was perplexed by something; I didn't feel nervous. Surely, I thought to myself, when I get to the class I'll feel nervous. Of *course* one will feel nervous in one's first class! I walked into the classroom, looked at the students scarcely younger than me, and felt completely at home. I've felt at home teaching ever since.

In the Fall of 1964, I began my formal academic career at the University of Toronto. Three years later I came to Trinity College in Hartford, Connecticut, where I have been teaching ever since, along with occasional forays teaching graduate seminars at The New School for Social Research, Boston University, and Suffolk University. Teaching, then, along with its inseparable components, scholarship and writing, have been my life's work. I want now to reflect on some of the experiences that have informed that work, or at least that core of it which is teaching. I shall not here join the debate over the merits of the "Socratic" teaching method versus the "teacher as dispenser of knowledge" model, a distinction which in any case I have always found artificial. Nor shall I engage in quasi-theoretical debates over any of the other "theories" of pedagogy. Rather, in a modest effort to respond to Socrates' implicit command in his famous dictum, "The unexamined life is not worth living," I shall here recount some of the informing teaching experiences of my life and reflect on what I have learned from them. I do so in the hope that they are not entirely idiosyncratic, and so that others may find reflection on them worthwhile.

I. Skiing and Being

There have been several teaching experiences that have been seminal to all the rest of my teaching, setting the standards for what I seek to accomplish. The first, and much the most decisive, was an experimental educational program I developed in 1969 at Trinity College and continued for three years. Though I had originally entitled it "Human Being, Play, and Nature," the students, with more imagination and panache, quickly dubbed it with the title by which it became known: "Skiing and Being." The conditions which led me to develop that program perhaps bear rehearsing.

I came to Trinity as a twenty-eight-year-old assistant professor in the Fall of 1967, after beginning my professional career for three years at the University of Toronto. Though I was happy to be at a prestigious liberal arts college, the kind of school where I guessed I would find the sorts of students I wanted to teach, it was not long before I began to sniff trouble. On campuses throughout the country at that time, two phenomena were converging that together, I soon concluded, made getting students to study and think about what they were studying virtually impossible on American campuses. These were, on the one hand, the politics of confrontation, whose most visible but by no means most troublesome manifestations were the various "sit-ins" around the country (Trinity students then prided themselves on having one of the first), and second, the drug culture so pervasive at that time. My difficulties with the latter were what finally drove me, in desperation, to develop what became the most powerful educational experience of my life, and according to most of the student participants, of theirs as well. Here is an example of the difficulties faced by teachers in those days.

In the Spring semester of 1968, I offered an upper-level seminar on phenomenology. My idea was that it would be primarily a research seminar that would give to the students perhaps their first experience of "phenomenological research." Accordingly, I would spend the first third or so of the course on a concentrated introduction to phenomenology, focusing on Husserl, Merleau-Ponty, and Sartre. As the students gradually gained a sense of what phenomenology is, they were each to develop a phenomenological research project on which they were to work, and present occasional progress reports to the class, for the rest of the term. This was to culminate in a major paper, their phenomenological research project.

The early part of the course, which I tightly controlled by lecturing most of the time, went pretty much as planned. The trouble began when I had more or less finished my lectures, and the students were to submit their project proposals, begin working on them, and make interim reports. One student, the only African American in the class, proposed what I initially thought was the best project in the class: a phenomenology of jazz. I responded with enthusiasm, noted that there was already a book on the phenomenology of dance to which he might refer for help, and in the ensuing weeks I began to educate myself on contemporary jazz, listening to music by John Coltrane, Pharoah Sanders, Archie

Shepp, and others, and reading what I could find on jazz, especially the writings of Nat Hentoff.

Several weeks later, the time came for the first of "Walter's" (so I'll call him) interim reports. Plausibly, he indicated that he'd want to play some music at his presentation, and would I please reserve a music room at the arts center, which I did. When I arrived at the music room the night of our seminar (it met one night per week for three hours), I found the students reclining around the room, some giggling, some in apparent reverie; there was an unmistakable odor of marijuana in the air. Trying to appear unperturbed, I sat down and indicated that Walter could begin.

"This is heavy music, man," he began in as thick "black talk" as this by no means poverty stricken young man could muster, "and we think that for you to appreciate it, you ought to turn on with us." Now, I was not about to "turn on" in class at that time in my life with a group of students whom I didn't entirely trust, so I responded lamely that the music was enough to turn me on. Walter then began by putting on a recording of Pharaoh Sanders, "The Creator Has A Master Plan." We all listened in silence, and at its conclusion, trying to be sensitive at once to the music and to phenomenological themes, I asked the class, "What did you think of the experience of time in that piece?" One student, who had listened lying on the floor with his eyes closed, leaned up briefly and, engaging a steadfast refusal to think, responded, "Man, you either dig it or you don't." He then returned to his reclined reverie.

At this point, in a show of what I was sure would be a successful display of righteous professorial indignation, I launched into an angry tirade on how they were wasting a special opportunity here, that they could turn on while listening to music any time in their rooms, that this was supposed to be a special occasion when they were to listen and *think* about the music, and that by coming to class "wasted" they had reduced what could have been an extraordinary experience of thoughtfulness to the everyday. I marched out of class in a dramatic huff.

Things seemed to improve for the next few weeks, or so I believed, while other students in the seminar gave for the most part more orthodox interim reports. Finally, toward the end of the semester, as students were taking turns presenting their final reports to the class, it came time for "Walter's" final presentation on the phenomenology of jazz. Again he requested the listening room in the art center, and again I reserved it and told the class to meet there on the evening of the next seminar.

On the appointed occasion I arrived at class with no intimation of what was to come. But it did not take me long to find out. The students were obviously already sky high, and not, as I was soon to learn, just on marijuana. Nevertheless, I asked "Walter" to begin. He played a piece of John Coltrane's. As I listened, I perused the record jacket "Walter" had given me, and noted a reference to Coltrane's "demise" that I did not at the time understand. At the conclusion of the piece, to break the literally stoned silence, I asked "how did Coltrane die?" "Walter," who so far in this, his major presentation of the seminar, had not yet risen from his reclined posture on the floor or opened his eyes, finally leaned up from the floor, looked at me condescendingly, and replied, "Man, did you ever hear of 'Om'?" My next few questions were met with no intelligible response, until finally, one of the students, who happened to be a leading campus radical and, I was to learn only later and too late, a major campus drug dealer, commented that this room wasn't conducive to listening or talking about such music appropriately, so why didn't we all come back to his room for the rest of the seminar?

Only a neophyte of consummate naivete could have agreed to such a thing, but I qualified in spades. Acknowledging that this was a nice gesture, I acceded, and we all trudged the hundred yards or so to "Steve's" room which, I discovered to my shock, was already absolutely crammed with people crazed on every manner of drug—truly a drug orgy of the sort I would have thought existed only in the hysterical imaginations of fearful conservatives. My most vivid image of the scene was of a young woman clad only in an American Flag, which she would occasionally undrape and stomp on while screaming epithets about American imperialism. Realizing that I had been duped, I announced as loudly as I could that the seminar would return to the music room, and promptly left the party for the music center, arming myself for the indignant speech to end all indignant speeches. Out of a class of, as I recall, eighteen students, one, an older graduate student, returned to class.

I relate this story because it was the most extreme case that happened to me that semester. Had it been the only one, I might have put it aside as an aberration. But it was the extreme of many less turbulent instances of students showing up to class high on drugs, or drunk, or trying to turn the class into a radical consciousness-raising session. The result was that at the end of the term I was one disillusioned young assistant professor. I began contemplating another career.

The Dean of the Faculty at Trinity at the time was a young physicist named Robert Fuller, a man so eccentric, in the opinion of many so loony, that he was dubbed by faculty wits "Roger Ram-jet." To me, he proved a great blessing; indeed, in terms of my career as a teacher, a savior. Lamenting to him the sorry state of American education, I allowed that I was becoming skeptical that it was any longer possible to get students on college campuses to think seriously or even care about the issues that moved me. In response to his query as to what it would take to correct the situation, I developed, thinking more or less out loud, the notion that I would have to take the students off the campus—the locus of all the distractions—and isolate them somewhere where I could subject them to what I was sure were the joys of philosophy without the superficial but more sensational distractions of the campus. That could be done, I continued, if I took about 15 students and had them take their entire workload for the semester, four courses, from me. I in turn would teach only them but teach them their entire semester's course load. That way, both the students and I would have our normal work assignments (actually I would have something of an overload), but in such a way that neither they nor I would have to remain on campus any longer. I could take them off somewhere and, I hoped, get them to think. Fuller's reply, to my shocked delight, was, "go ahead."

So began what was to prove the most powerful educational experience of my life. Today, of course, such a proposal would have to be presented formally to the curriculum committee and several deans. I doubt very much if it would ever be passed. But in those simpler days, I needed only the approval of a wild and crazy Dean of the Faculty. It was up to me to withstand the occasionally scandalized grumbling of a number of my colleagues in other departments.

I developed a fairly elaborate four course syllabus centered around the themes of human being and play, human being and nature. The program was interdisciplinary before its time. The readings included lots of Plato, Nietzsche, Heidegger, and Sartre, but also figures as wide-ranging as Freud, Homer, Thomas Mann, Knute Hamsun, Robert Frost, and Richard Wagner. (Not the least of the scandalized grumbling came from a few colleagues in the Classics, Psychology, English, and Music departments, who wondered what warrant I had to teach material that was clearly "not philosophy," in fact, that "belonged" to them). In addition to the work we did together, each student had to develop an independent project on a topic related to our guiding themes, which would then be presented to the group later in the year. Many students did art projects, others did dance performances, some wrote poetry, or did musical performances. One industrious group made a film about the program. A theater major wrote a play.

Each year of the next three I rented a large old house somewhere in Vermont from January through March. The college room costs from which the students were freed by living away from the campus were pooled to pay for our lodging. Their board money went toward our meal costs. This proved more than ample. My plan was to be in Vermont for those three winter months, when most of our intensive studying would take place, then return to the campus after Spring Vacation, so that for the last five weeks of the semester each student could write a master's thesis-length paper on a topic germane to our study. As it turned out, some of those papers were better than many master's theses.

I want to describe something of our day to day lives while in Vermont, then reflect on what happened pedagogically during the three remarkable semesters that I participated in this project. I should mention first that, particularly in the first year, the group of students who enlisted was not a cohort of the most high-powered intellectuals on the campus. They probably signed on in large measure because of the opportunities they knew the program would afford to do lots of skiing. But neither they nor I appreciated until much later just how radical a plan I had conceived, and how much it would change our lives.

For openers, the program was born in controversy, and the students knew that as well as I did. Many colleagues, as I've already mentioned, regarded it as a scandal, as did many of the participants' parents. We were all under considerable pressure to make sure this worked. If we couldn't prove it an educational success, it would never happen again. Second, no one anticipated the powerful effects of the relative isolation I had constructed. In addition to the students, my wife, Anne, and our two children, Christopher and Craig, were part of the experience. In the first year, Chris was four, Craig all of three months old. Also in that first year, Trinity was still almost entirely a male college, and all the students along were male. One, however, was married with a wife and infant son, both of whom participated as well. So in addition to the students, we had two young families along. In the two subsequent years, as Trinity became more fully coeducational, the students were fairly evenly split among men and women. I had only one firm social rule, one perhaps understandable in the light of the conditions that led to my conceiving the program, and also in the light of the habit of the local Vermont police of barging into our house in blithe inattention to constitutional constraints against unwarranted search: no drugs.

Neither Anne nor Lindsay Stewart, the other young mother in the program, were about to take on the project of mothering 15 or so college students in addition to their own children. A fairly elaborate set of job assignments had to be distributed, everything from buying and cooking the food to dish washing, house cleaning, and garbage detail, which involved several trips daily to the town dump. At first, we simply drew lots to see who got what jobs each week. But Anne and I soon recognized that having particularly responsible students in certain jobs was crucial to the functioning of the household. We began fixing the lots.

To take care of our play needs, and to give us a common play experience—after all, that was one of the themes of the semester—I obtained a special ski lift rate at a local ski area, good for weekdays only. This had two interesting consequences. First, since the lift tickets weren't valid on weekends and since the students had all week to ski anyway, the weekends became a period of intense studying. Second, since they could ski any weekday, and since, in any case, I gave, shall we say, challenging reading assignments, the students soon realized that it was both inappropriate and unnecessary to ski all day or even half a day on any given day. The typical drill became for the students to study through the morning and early afternoon, then, about 2:00 P.M. or so, a carload or two of students—and often Anne and I—would head for the slopes, take a couple of runs, then return for dinner: our "daily workout" as it were. But they were not merely our workouts, our "extra-curricular activities," to use a term that has become virtually one of condescension. Since one of the themes of the semester was the relation of human being and play, our shared skiing time gave us a common play experience to accompany our common reading syllabus, one to which we could all knowledgeably appeal.

Four nights a week, Monday through Thursday, we had seminars, beginning around 7:00 P.M. and rarely ending before 11:00 P.M., without a break. These were the only seminars in my teaching career in which the students did not require a break (and that in a *three*-hour seminar) at some point. I attribute this to the remarkable intensity that our sessions took on, which I shall address in a moment. Everyone seemed to understand that a break would interrupt the flow of the seminar. As it was, by 11:00 or so we were drained and exhausted; typically, some of us would have a beer, and we'd go to bed.

Several interesting consequences, some anticipated, some unanticipated, followed from our living situation. One delightful unanticipated one had to do with a certain implicit pressure to work. Each year, there was one large living room where many of us did our reading and preparation. Occasionally, students reported, they would come down into the room prepared to "goof off" or perhaps "blow off" the morning's work. There I and several other students would be, busily preparing for the night's seminar. This would usually bring about a quick change of plans in favor of scholarly diligence.

In a similar vein, because it was the same group of students night after night at seminar, we soon came to know each other extremely well. If ever a student were poorly prepared for the night's seminar, it would be painfully obvious to all. Needless to say, "cutting" a class was out of the question.

But much more positive things happened as well. At the beginning of each year, I passed out a detailed syllabus of the reading assignments for each seminar, which did indeed become the basis of each night's discussion. But because it was the same group of people studying the same material night after night, it soon became easy and natural to relate material from last night's or last week's seminar to the issue at hand. The detailed syllabus notwithstanding, the seminars soon blended together so that on any occasion, anything from any previous seminar could be drawn into the discussion, and all present would know what was at stake. The fact that all of us were studying the same material in all four "courses" enabled the whole to take on an interdisciplinary character far beyond what I had hoped, and far beyond what I have seen since.

Surely the most special quality of the program, however, was the remarkable intensity that our sessions took on, matched by nothing I have done in education since then. No doubt many factors contributed to this. The living situation—fifteen students and a young family all in one house—was itself intense enough. Back at campus, if one person became irritated at another, it was easy simply to ignore or avoid the irritating party. Here, it was imperative to face the problem and deal with it. In addition, especially in the more coeducational second and third years and understandably in this situation, romantic involvements among the students tended to wax and wane with a passion accentuated by the intimacy of the living situation. (It has been observed to me by several former participants that I am here understating the matter. As one years later said to me, "Drew, you have no idea!") In the seminars themselves, basic positions soon were taken by different people in such a way that the next night's reading deepened and expanded the debate. Conflicts of interpretation, instead of rising and dissipating in one evening, tended to be sustained through weeks of regular dialogue. Each night, it seemed, with some new reading under our belts, the discussion was rejoined on expanded turf.

Each year's group was unique and the pedagogical lessons I learned from the experience varied accordingly. In the first year, we rented an old farmhouse along a country road near Londonderry, Vermont, dubbed by its owner "Unserhaus." That first year's group, as I've already mentioned, was not composed primarily of conventionally excellent students. It was all the more exhilarating to see these not highly motivated students begin to get genuinely involved with the ideas and texts we considered. Many of these students, had we been back on campus, almost certainly would not have taken their courses very seriously. Yet here they were genuinely engaged by often difficult and demanding material, engaged in ways that I suspected—and they later admitted—had not happened before. I gained that year some sense of the enormous affect that one's educational environment has over student performance. The contrast between what I then regarded as the deplorable environment back at the college and the wonderful success of this more isolated environment taught me once and for all never to be satisfied with an educational situation in which students were not encouraged to take their studies seriously. This lesson came home to me with special force by what some might suppose to be a negative example. One student, Jon Goodwin, was so moved by our experience that he decided that, since this was what education *ought* to be like, and since neither Trinity nor any other college could match it, continuing an inferior college education was hardly worthwhile. He withdrew from Trinity never to return, and now makes an ample living as the most thoughtful sign painter in the state of New Hampshire, farming in the summer with his family to augment their income.

The second year was strikingly different. Still controversial but with the clear success of the previous year, the program attracted a group of genuinely gifted students. Of the fifteen students that year, at least three went on to get Ph.D's in philosophy, another in English, several became doctors. We rented the carriage house behind a hotel called "The Bavarian Castle" in Proctorsville, Vermont. A number of factors contributed to making this second year an even more powerful experience than the first. Certainly, the penetrating intellectual ability of the students was a factor. But so, surely, was the fact that the group was now more or less evenly divided between men and women. That made the intimate living conditions all the more complicated, but also deeper, and often more hilarious. At least one marriage eventuated from that winter, and a lot of other things besides. Whatever the factors, nothing before or since in my teaching experience has matched the depth and intensity of those seminars. This was occasionally brought home to me by the astonishment of a few of our guest speakers. I recall one evening when a colleague from Bates College who had written a book on play came to observe our program. On his first night there, we had a particularly passionate debate about whether Socratic self-knowledge was an unmitigated good or, as some students argued, a double-edged sword, as likely to make one miserable as happy. At the end of the seminar, a few of us, no doubt to release the tension of the seminar, went outside into a fresh snowstorm, and began engaging in a roughhouse form of play which I had dubbed "piling" (it might be described as a boisterous introduction to the joys of contact improvisational dance). My colleague watched all this in astonishment, then, instead of joining in the fun, ran over to me and began asking me what I had done to establish this kind of close relationship with my students. Here we were, releasing our energies after an especially passionate seminar, covered with snow and laughing hysterically, and I was being interviewed about my teaching techniques! I think it was then that I stopped having much regard for a great emphasis on pedagogical technique.

My first two books, one on the presocratics and one on Plato, and much of the spirit of the third, on play, arose out of those discussions. Night after night, everything seemed to hang on our understanding the issue at hand properly. The debates were sometimes fierce, but usually, eventually, positive. I remember that one of the best of those students (now a professor of philosophy), who understood the difficult texts we were studying with a thoroughness few could match, argued passionately against the efficacy of "book learning," unfazed by the self-referential objections leveled by some of his peers. At least half a dozen of the long papers written by those students would have been superior to most master's theses. Perfecting a tradition begun the previous year, our last evening in Vermont before Spring vacation was devoted to an all-night banquet, all of us, men, women, and children, dressed in makeshift Greek robes.

That year I began to realize that the intimacy of the living situation and the intensity of the educational experience were of a piece. Years later, when I helped coach the women's basketball team for a while, I saw something of that intensity develop in the women athletes, occasioned there, I suspect, by the fact that their whole selves, body, mind, and soul, were invested in what they were doing. Here in Vermont, the total involvement in the experience, both during the seminars and outside of them, made possible the same intensity. I came to realize that in the more orthodox environments of liberal arts colleges, that depth of commitment and experience will only rarely be achieved in an isolated classroom. Every teacher knows how exhilarating it is to see a student take on the passion for understanding and learning that informs the teacher's life. But every teacher also knows how difficult that commitment is to establish, especially in isolation. If students are asked to focus only their intellect, not their entire selves, on a given subject for three classroom hours or so per week plus a few extra hours for the reading assignment, and if their other courses, much less their broader lives on campus, are at best tangentially related to the subject of the course, then only so much commitment—and not all that much—can be expected. The kind of passionate immersion in the material that we all hope our students will experience, and which the students in Vermont and the athletes I coached surely did experience, is a function in part of a certain totality of immersion. When a given course remains discretely different from one's other studies and from one's life as a whole, the commitment and the investment of passion in that course will be as fragmented as the environment in which it takes place. That is why few things are as important on a college campus as establishing a total atmosphere of genuine involvement in learning. Only insofar as the entire college environment can take on something of that immersive whole we found in Vermont and I found in the athletes I coached will a similar experience be achieved on campus.

The third year of the program was quite different from the first two, and in many ways the strangest. We again rented an old house in Vermont and began our "Skiing and Being" semester early in January. My family again came along, Chris now in first grade, Craig a toddler. Anne again, as she had the previous years, added to the richness of the experience by doing her own pottery work at the house and inviting the students to participate. The students, amused by the name of the town to which Nietzsche's Zarathustra comes to teach, (*Thus Spoke Zarathustra* was part of our syllabus) painted a large sign which they hung on the front of the house, proclaiming to skeptical local citizens its name: "The Motley Cow." It was, once again, a memorable semester.

But something was distinctly different, and before long I made a guess as to what it was. In the first two years the program was steeped in controversy as I have already mentioned, and the students understood full well that a burden was on them to make this work. They responded wonderfully. But now, after two years, the program was something of a sensation. Word of its success, of its truly bizarre mixture of learning and fun, was spreading through and beyond the Trinity community. The Hartford Courant had devoted a large spread to it. Even the renowned German philosopher, Martin Heidegger, was informed of it on the streets of Freiburg by an enthusiastic participant (*"Sehr gemütlich,"* I'm told, was his response). The program had become, in its own way, respectable. And that brought about, I thought, a subtle but decisive change in the attitude of the students. Whereas the previous years' students had come with the burden and resolve to make the program work, the students now were coming here to enjoy the fruits of this successful program. The recognition that they had to create the success of the program themselves had been diminished. (I should state that I am not talking about every individual student, some of whom were truly outstanding, but about a prevalent attitude that informed the group). The consequences of this subtle change were striking, at least to me. To be sure, the program was a great educational and experiential success. But something of the cohesiveness, something of the passionate involvement in a project experienced as common, was lost. Some students began going back to the campus on weekends—something that had almost never happened in the first two years. One student even missed a seminar or two, ostensibly because of romantic troubles back on campus. I occasionally had the sense that some of them were not especially well-prepared for this or that seminar.

As I write this, I'm struck by the humor of reacting so strongly, even some twenty years later, to what are, after all everyday occurrences in the lives of those of us who teach. But that in itself is perhaps the lesson. In that third year, the program was becoming "normalized." It was losing that sense of being a precarious and controversial experiment that demanded strong commitment from its participants, and no amount of exhortation on my part succeeded in reestablishing it. The semester was a genuine success, but something had been lost.

This poses, I think, a great challenge for those of us who teach on college campuses, where, for the most part, the sense of tradition, continuity, and repetition from year to year is stronger than the sense of change, controversy, and unique opportunity. How can we generate in our students and in ourselves again and again, year after year, that sense of controversy, challenge, experiment, even of precariousness and personal responsibility, that so informed the first two years of "Skiing and Being" and made those years so unique? In a sense, our own good intentions tend toward just the opposite. Trinity, like most colleges, has a freshman orientation period each August, and I am often struck by how remarkably successful it is. In almost no time, it seems, most of the freshmen are made to feel comfortable and secure. I wonder if we don't succeed all too well. Comfort and security surely were not the stuff of "Skiing and Being." In those first two years especially, we lived, played, and thought, precariously. And it was fun.

II. Philosophy of Sport

The second defining teaching experience for me was the development and teaching of a course which I have taught for almost twenty years now, entitled "Philosophy of Sport." Again, the conditions which led me first to offer this course some twenty years ago and repeatedly since then are an important clue to what I wanted to accomplish and what I found worthwhile therein.

From childhood on, I was very active athletically. Although always of rather small stature, I did have certain athletic gifts which both aided me in and led me to my involvement in sports: quickness, agility, and a highly competitive nature. Like most young kids, I began by playing whatever was available that day, but as time went on, basketball became my favorite sport, in part, no doubt, because in those days basketball was the king of sports in Philadelphia, where I grew up. By the time I was in seventh grade and had my first opportunity to play in formal interscholastic sports, it was clear that, despite my small stature, I had a "future" in the game, and I began to commit myself totally to the sport. By "commit myself totally," I mean this: with the exception of at most four or five days per year, I played basketball for several hours every single day, no matter what the season. Cold winter weekends proved no obstacle; as I grew through high school, my like-minded friends and I grew adept at sneaking into the various college gymnasia throughout the city. When a janitor found us in one gym and kicked us out, we would simply move on to the next. To this day, when I return to one Philadelphia college or another to participate in a conference, my first recollection of the place is invariably the old gym (by now often replaced by a fancy new one) and the youthful memories it had for me.

All this commitment gradually paid its natural dividends, and I became a very good basketball player. I was the "star" of the team in high school, made the all-county team and played on any number of all-star teams. Fortunately for me, my parents had a strong commitment to educational excellence, and made it a condition of my continued playing that I make the honor roll each semester. This, but certainly not any inherent interest in my high school studies, led me to do well in school. I recall that this was not a very time-consuming effort. One of the colleges that recruited me my senior year was Princeton University, where one of my best friends, also a basketball player, had enrolled the year before. In the Fall of 1957, I enrolled at Princeton to begin my college basketball career and, as it turned out, my education.

My four years at Princeton were defining ones, as so often is the case with one's college years. For the first time, I had teachers who showed me that there was something at stake in the books we read, something at once important and tremendously exciting: ideas. My interest in my studies gradually shifted from parentally induced coercion to intrinsic enthusiasm. I majored in philosophy, initially, I told myself and my parents, as good preparation for law school. But by my senior year I knew that I wanted to go on to an academic career. My special philosophic interest was Greek Philosophy, and especially the dialogues of Plato, where philosophy was portrayed as arising out of the exigencies of lived experience, and where Socrates assured us that self-knowledge and the question of the best life was the guiding issue of philosophy, and so that "the unexamined life was not worth living."

Meanwhile, and for me at the time still decisive, my basketball career continued to flourish. In those days, freshmen were ineligible for varsity competition and had a separate "freshman" team. Ours was a very good one; we became fast friends, and in the ensuing years became the core of Princeton's championship teams of that era. At the end of the season, to my delight and honor, I was elected team captain.

My three years on the varsity were enjoyable and deeply meaningful. In my sophomore year, led largely by four senior players, we tied for the Ivy League Championship. In my junior and senior years, as my own class became the core of the team, we won the championship outright. In my senior year, after winning the league championship, we got as far as the Quarterfinals of the NCAA tournament, now popularly called the "Sweet Sixteen," where we finally lost. That was, I believe, the farthest an Ivy League team had ever gone at the time. We were a very good team.

More than that, we had become a team of profound friendships. We were almost all club mates in the same "eating club," (Princeton's substitute for fraternities). Three of the players were my roommates; a fourth, my brother, now a sophomore soon to become an all-league basketball player and an all-American lacrosse player. Through the kinship of the game and through that ineffable quality that coaches call "chemistry," we developed friendships deeper than I had ever known, and as deep as any I have known since. We learned together all the lessons usually and rightly ascribed to sports: teamwork, self-discipline, that in sports hustling and having fun are proportional to each other, gracious winning, dealing with defeat. We learned about the art museums at the various cities we visited to play games. Most of all, we learned about ourselves. Virtually my entire self-identity was tied up in this activity. If anyone had asked me at the time, "Who are you?", I would have had no trouble answering: "I'm a basketball player."

So I lived this double life as a budding intellectual and a varsity athlete, and I was quite content with it. Only later, in graduate school, did it dawn on me that there was something decisively wrong with this diremption. Here I had devoted a monumental amount of time to this athletic activity (certainly far more time than I had ever devoted to my studies), had devoted an equal amount of physical and psychological energy to it, virtually my entire self-identity was tied up with it, yet not once at this great institution of higher learning did a single one of my teachers ever suggest to me that there was something to think about here. Neither in class nor outside of class was it ever suggested to me that there was material for thoughtful reflection in my athletic involvement, that there was a rich opportunity here to join together my athletic and intellectual lives in a thoughtful reflection on the meaning of my involvement in basketball. I sometimes joke that the closest my academic and athletic lives ever came to each other was when a professor would occasionally ask me for tickets to a big game. It should be emphasized, incidentally, that Princeton was in no way unusual in this regard. The very term used to describe athletics, "extra-curricular activities,"—not to mention the low esteem usually accorded to "physical education"—testifies clearly enough to our cultural decision that athletic activity is essentially to be excluded from the heart of our educational lives.

Only when I was in graduate school at Penn State University did the occasion arise at last for me to explicitly bring these two informing domains together. In a seminar on the thought of Martin Heidegger, our major paper assignment was to give a Heideggerian phenomenological description of some important personal experience. I chose the last four minutes of my last basketball game at Princeton—the one where we lost in the NCAA Quarterfinals by a point or two—described it at length, then gave a Heideggerian analysis of it in which I criticized certain aspects of Heidegger's position as inadequate to the richness of that experience.

I thought that the job was now done. I had joined together what had wrongfully been kept asunder, and now I could move on to other things. My professor, Richard Gottshalk, was much more insightful when he handed back my paper with the comment, "You'll never live down the fact that you played basketball." He was right, for what I had begun with that paper was a habit of reflection which finally tried to be true to the Socratic dictum regarding the examined life, a habit of reflection which has since resulted in two books and dozens of articles on the meaning and significance of play.

As I began my teaching career, I did not want what had happened to me to happen to my own students who were athletes. I didn't want them to be forced to say what I had to say, that not one of my professors ever suggested to me that there was something to think about here. Accordingly, shortly after I came to Trinity College, I developed a course which I entitled simply "Philosophy of Sport." Again, as with "Skiing and Being," it met with considerable skepticism if not cynicism from some colleagues, but again I was undaunted. I was by then thoroughly convinced that there was much that was genuinely thought provoking in athletic activity, much that could be made the legitimate matter for philosophic thought. Since then I have offered the course at least every other year since the early 1970's, and always I have to close enrollments to limit the size. Not surprisingly, many of the students who take the course are intercollegiate athletes.

I can rehearse briefly the sorts of issues we take up in the course. Because many of the students are committed athletes and take the course out of a basically positive experience of sport, I typically begin with the most radical critique of sport that I can find. Usually this is a Marxian critique based on the supposedly inevitable alienation and exploitation that accompanies competitive activity, beginning with economic activity and moving from there to any other competitive activity. I offer this critique to the students as a challenge to which, if they want to thoughtfully continue to affirm their involvement in athletics, they must be able to respond. I then move on to issues surrounding the relation of sport and society. Often in this section I focus on the issues of racism and sexism in sport. The narrower and more delimited domain of sport often gives these social problems a clarity of focus that is more difficult to achieve in the larger and murkier realm of society at large. From here, we move on to raise a set of ethical issues in sport, which can range from elemental issues of adherence to rules, to abuses in college athletics, to some of the problems in the proscription of performance enhancing drugs.

From here we often turn to the question of self-knowledge in sport, which I can approach from several standpoints. One might be called the psychoanalytic approach. There are books which enable the students to ask what they can learn about themselves through reflection on their choice of sport (e.g., team or individual sports, competitive or non-competitive, contact or non-contact, etc.) as well as their mode of involvement in sport (poor losers, "clutch" players, etc.). A second approach uses the Zen standpoint to reflect on the deeper meaning of athletic involvement. A number of books are available on this theme, often entitled something like "Zen _____" (fill in the name of your favorite sport). I usually conclude this section with a consideration of the Socratic sense of self-knowledge; what can we learn about our possibilities and our limits, what we know and what we don't know, from our involvement in sport?

From here we often turn to that set of issues surrounding the nature of embodiment. What better arena than athletic activity to address the relative strengths of dualistic approaches to human being ("mind and body"), the phenomenological construal of the "lived body," or physicalist interpretations of our nature? Especially in connection with the phenomenological approach, we can raise issues of the experience of spatiality and temporality in sport which are often revelatory.

A host of other issues usually find their way into the course; the place and meaning of aesthetics in sport, the experience of finitude therein, definitional questions regarding such terms as "sport," "game," "athletics," or "play." I usually close with the development of some views of my own regarding what I call the "stance of play," in which we reflect on the stance or orientation we take when we play and how that differs from our more ordinary, non-play situations.

What is striking about this course, that might shed some light on the project of teaching? First and foremost, I think, is the experiential element in play, and therefore in a course on the topic. When I teach a course, say, on Kant's *Critique of Pure Reason*, or Hegel's *Phenomenology of Spirit*, I often must first persuade the students that something is at stake here, that something is addressed in these books that matters, or ought to matter, to them as they live their lives. No one who turns for the first time to Kant or Hegel is an "expert" on the issues addressed therein. Yet in a very real sense, almost all the students in the Philosophy of Sport come to the course as "experts" on the issues we study. Almost all of them have already had an extensive, intense, and often profound experience of those issues. They can appeal to their own experience to evaluate what is said in the books we read and the judgments we put forth. I suspect this is part of the reason why so many students find the course such an important and moving one. It appeals directly to their experience and their passion.

That, I've learned from Philosophy of Sport, is a crucial propaedeutic to philosophic commitment, and I daresay, to intellectual commitment altogether. Particularly as American society and education has evolved, precious few students arrive at college as already committed intellectuals, devoted with passion to what is with a Cartesian dualistic prejudice called the "life of the mind." The first task, the introductory task, of the teacher is to show the students, as a few of my own teachers showed me, that the ideas developed in books do address our lives, that they are at once exciting and worthy of our passionate commitment. If we succeed in that, their subsequent educations will be largely self-motivated. And the best way to accomplish this introduction is to appeal to their own experience, to show that the issues addressed can be and are drawn from that very experience. For passionately committed young athletes, a course such as the Philosophy of Sport can accomplish that introduction.

III. Coaching

It is a virtual cliche that coaches are or ought to be teachers. We testify to the insincerity of our belief in this bromide, however, when we regularly refuse to give anything like full course credit to "physical education" and refuse to accord coaches the status of full faculty members. But in the early 1970's, I had an opportunity for four memorable years to involve myself in coaching in such a way that

I learned what a deep and rich teaching occasion athletic coaching can be. The cliche as I experienced it is true in spades.

In 1970, Trinity College decided to become coeducational. In most academic departments, this required a gradual set of adjustments, including the effort to hire a significant number of women faculty, and the gradual introduction of appropriate new courses. But in the athletic department there was a special urgency. Not gradually but immediately opportunities for intercollegiate teams had to be established for women. Equally important, women had to be hired on the athletic staff, as coaches and role models. A squash and tennis coach was hired. It was decided to establish women's lacrosse, basketball, and field hockey teams as well. The athletic staff astutely hired a woman named Robin Sheppard, to coach these three sports. Robin was superbly qualified to coach field hockey and lacrosse (and indeed, ever since her hiring Trinity has had one championship team after another in those two sports). But by her own admission, she was a novice in basketball. Early in her first year at Trinity we were talking about her reservations regarding her ability to coach basketball, and in an effort to help, I suggested that I would come to two practices, one to do a "clinic" on offense, one on defense. I did so and I loved it. "Well," I suggested to Robin who heartily agreed, "why don't I keep on coming to practices whenever it's convenient?" I did that and continued to enjoy it thoroughly. As the first game approached, Robin and I decided that, since it was a home game, I might as well sit on the bench with her and help with the game coaching.

To make a long and enjoyable story short, soon I was attending virtually all the practices, all the home games, and as many of the away games as my teaching schedule allowed. For four years, until Trinity was able to expand the women's coaching staff and hire a fully qualified women's basketball coach, I served as Robin's assistant coach of women's basketball.

It was a remarkable four years. In trying to describe the experience to others, I have often suggested that it was like having an entire class of honors students, committed to learning as much as they can, willing to throw their whole selves into the activity, even to be consumed by it. To have a group of students impassioned to learn, willing to invest their whole selves into doing so, grateful for every step forward that you help them take, is a truly wonderful teaching situation, and that is what coaches often have.

I remember one notable exception, in the first year. The 1970's were a period of remarkable transition in women's sports. Until that time, for the most part, young women were socialized not to invest too much of themselves in sports. Some of them, athletically gifted, might indeed dabble in the sport, but certainly not with the passion that most young men invested in their athletic lives. I remember, for example, that Robin told me initially that it was typical in women's sports to practice only every other day. We changed that. As the first season wore on, we were preparing for a particularly important weekend game. Early in the week, our center came to Robin and me to inform us that she would not be at the game that weekend. "Why?" I asked in astonishment, since she had no injury. The answer: she had a date for Dartmouth's "Winter Carnival Weekend," and didn't want to miss it. That elicited from me an impassioned address to the team on the theme that they would only get out of an activity what they put into it, that as long as they merely dabbled in basketball their return would be mild at best, that if they really wanted the kind of depth and meaning from their sport that they saw their male counterparts experiencing, they had to invest a like amount of themselves in the activity. To say the least, my speech worked—they were obviously ready for such an invitation. Before long, Robin and I were warning them to control their emotions in games—some of them were ready to haul off and hit opposing players who angered them! At the end of one season, the student athletes gave me a plaque, which I cherish proudly to this day. It reads simply: "To Drew: Thanks for treating us like guys."

Every teacher knows how wonderful it is to have students who deeply care about their academic work (and not just for their grades!), who are willing to invest whatever time, energy, and even psychic identity is necessary into the project of improving their understanding. That is what every coach for the most part regularly has, and they should be thankful. What is it about sports that enables this to happen so often that it is virtually normal, whereas it is so difficult to achieve in the classroom? I offer this speculation. In almost any sport, the athlete's entire being is involved. Their intellects are engaged, certainly, though this is foolishly denied by the "dumb jock" myth; they must listen to the coach and learn the plays, strategies, fundamentals, etc. But obviously, their bodies are involved as well. Their intellects, bodies, and with them their passions and even their self-identities are all at stake in their efforts to improve, to play well. That totality of immersion strikes me as a fundamental element in the depth of commitment that so many athletes have to their sport. And it is precisely that totality which is so difficult to achieve in the academic sphere. How can we do so?

It will only rarely be achieved, I suggest, in isolated courses. As I argued in my discussion of "Skiing and Being," part of its success was that an environment was established in which the students' entire selves could be devoted to that project. This will always be difficult to achieve in a college atmosphere, where the students' academic lives, already too often separated from their social and "extra-curricular" lives, are themselves fragmented into different combinations of often unrelated courses. Nevertheless, my experiences with "Skiing and Being" and with coaching assure me that we must do all we can to establish academic communities which invite something approaching the totality of immersion that was so integral to those more focused projects. If we can successfully invite the students into that totality, Aristotle's dictum that "the beginning is half of the whole" will surely prove true, and the subsequent progress of their education will be relatively easy.

But what can the individual teacher in the isolated classroom do? My previous reflections have surely implied, not everything. But not everything is also not nothing. Presumably, most of us who are teachers have chosen this profession because, in one way or another, we have experienced that totality of immersion which we now seek to instill in our students. One thing we can surely do is *exhibit* that immersion ourselves in our classrooms, exhibit it enthusiastically, passionately, indeed if we can, seductively. It has struck me over the years that when students say kind things about my teaching, it often has to do with the contagious enthusiasm for ideas that I exhibit in the classroom. Especially as they graduate and move on in life, what they seem to remember most of my teaching is less my interpretation of the "Cave Analogy" in the *Republic* or of Nietzsche's doctrine of the *Übermensch*, and more the openness and passion of my commitment to philosophy, to the reflective clarification of human experience. I think I know why. They sense, even if only later, that once they were themselves committed, they were fully capable of thinking through for themselves the specifics of this or that theory or issue. They needed me simply to put them on the way. What Plato says of philosophy in his "Seventh Letter" is I think true of almost everything we teach. It must be developed over "a long period of dwelling together concerning the subject itself and living together with it, when suddenly, like a light kindled by a leaping spark, it comes to be in the soul and at once becomes self-nourishing." (*Letters* 7.341d; my translation). We who teach must strive to be that leaping spark.

Addendum

Fall, 2021: I have now been retired from formal teaching for some five years. As I reflect back on what I here wrote some years ago, a number of themes seem to me to call for expansion.

At one point in my discussion of "Skiing and Being," I refer with perhaps ill-concealed bemusement to a colleague who questioned me about my "teaching methods." Since that time, to say the least, an emphasis on "teaching methodology" has flourished. Through the years, I have been "invited" (those are sneer quotes) to almost yearly workshops on teaching methodology. I have learned about the importance of "rubrics." I have been assured of the importance of "measurement of outcomes." I have watched my now fully grown son, with some 20 years of successful elementary school teaching under his belt, be gifted with "coaches," young people fresh out of education schools and often with almost no classroom teaching under their belts, who enter his classroom to inform him of the latest in teaching techniques that should inform his teaching.

I remain a skeptic. Almost all the rubrics and outcome measurement techniques to which I have been subjected strike me as, in the end, claiming to quantify the unquantifiable. A brief story: towards the end of my career at Trinity, it was decided by the administration that each department should define for itself the overarching "teaching goal" of their department, after which they would have to work out how to measure that outcome. The philosophy department thought we had come up with the perfect *reductio ad absurdum* of such a project. We announced to the dean that our overarching goal was "to make our students more thoughtful." Our implicit message was "try to quantify that!" "Excellent!," came the reply from the dean's office; "Now work out the outcome measurement rubrics." Fortunately, I retired before having to indulge in this insanity.

We should have learned from the decades long experiment with "SAT's" as a "measurement" of students' aptitude for college work. The evidence is now in: SAT's are very poor predictors of student success in college and student success after college. The one thing they predict well? Social class! If you have the family wealth to pay for a special class in SAT taking, or go to a prestigious school that "teaches to the test," you'll do very well. If not, probably not. Is that the basis on which we want to select our undergraduate students? More and more schools, including some of the most prestigious, are therefore no longer requiring SAT's. A plausible first step.

Second, the denigration of Physical Education of which I complained then (the very phrase indicates that it has something to do with *education*) continues apace. Concomitantly, our profound ambivalence about the place of sports in education persists. High schools and colleges are still the primary locus of organized preprofessional sports, although especially in "Division I" sports and thus at many large universities, the connection of sports to the education of the student athletes remains tenuous at best. Coaches retiring after long, successful careers are invariably praised for being "great teachers," although there is no clamor to make coaches full faculty members. I suspect that few educational theorists today still would buy into Descartes' radical distinction between the mind and the body and no less radical identification of who we are with our minds. Yet most colleges still exhibit fully this Cartesian dualism in their curricula, relegating physical education and sports to "extra-curricular" status in favor of what is still called "the life of the mind." I'm reminded in this regard of an event that occurred in the early days of co-education at Trinity. There arose a strong movement to establish a department of dance in the college (this had the unanimous and enthusiastic support of the Philosophy Department). At the faculty meeting where the proposal was debated, one faculty member spoke against the proposal on the grounds that dance had "too much to do with the body." He was a member of the Biology Department. Dance was eventually established as the Department of Theater and Dance, in part because the Philosophy Department threatened to rename itself as "the Department of Philosophy and Dance." Judy Dworin, the founder and long-time chair of that Department, still laughs with me about that, and we wonder whether it might not have been a better idea to establish what would have been our unique joint department. I still occasionally imagine a "Department of Philosophy and Dance," whose motto might be a quote from Nietzsche's Zarathustra: "I could only believe in a god who could dance."

One final observation: in most European countries, sports are not tied closely to formal education. The best soccer teams in Europe do not play for the Sorbonne, Oxford, or Cambridge. Instead, in an implicit acknowledgement that there is no interesting connection between sport and education, sports organizations are separated from educational institutions into separate "clubs," where men and women of all ages have the opportunity to participate in this or that sport. To be sure, there are important benefits to this organizational principle. But we in America have traditionally tied our sports teams closely to our educational institutions, from middle school through high school to college. Only at the professional level are the two separated. Such a structure *seems* to affirm that we see an important *educational* element in sports. Yet once we do so, we too often implicitly *deny* that claim by relegating our sports teams to "extra-curricular activities" and denying full professorial status to our coaches. In my judgment, that ambivalence is regrettable.

CHAPTER 2

On Being a Basketball Player

But yield who will to their separation,
My object in living is to unite
My avocation and my vocation
As my two eyes make one in sight.
Only where love and need are one
And the work is play for mortal stakes,
Is the deed ever really done
For Heaven and the future's sakes.

ROBERT FROST, "TWO TRAMPS IN MUD TIME."

IT HAPPENED AGAIN YESTERDAY. At the start of each academic year, a group of faculty and staff at the college agree to come down to the gym at noon twice a week for a basketball game. It was the first game of the year, but for some reason I had one of those days, more and more rare now, when the memory of my former skills for one last time served me well. After missing my first couple of shots, I began to make one after another, and before long I found myself in one of those indescribable experiences of confidence that every shot would go in, that I could *feel* as I went up for a shot that

36

everything was right. It was as if I *knew* the ball would go in because the ball became less an object external to my body that I had to control than an extension of my hands, perhaps more, even an extension of my will. On the few occasions when I missed, I would stare momentarily at the basket in honest disbelief, astonished that such a thing could happen. At the end of the workout and for the rest of the day, I felt a sense of satisfaction and fulfillment that few experiences can match in its immediacy and totality. "I can still do this," I thought, "I'm still a basketball player." Here I am, an academic in my late fifties, blessed with teaching and academic awards, successful in my publishing career, and the fact that I had hit a few jump shots at lunch had made my day.

How does it happen that a given activity becomes so decisive in one's life that it begins to count not just as one of the activities one enjoys, perhaps even an important one, but as definitive of one's being, and especially definitive of one's self-identity? For many of us, that sense of self-identity in the light of a given activity comes only with the arrival at adulthood and the choice of a career. One "becomes" an artist, teacher, doctor, and begins to think of oneself in those terms. But for many athletes and certainly for me, the event of self-identity with athletics takes place much, much earlier.

How did I "become" a basketball player in that strong self-identifying sense at such a young age, and why would basketball have become my sport? I stand here, at my full growth, a towering 5'8". Until seventh grade, I was the smallest *person* in my grade, girl or boy. In the ninth grade, the wrestling coach, noting my growing enthusiasm for the game, encouraged me to come out for wrestling instead, where my stature would not be such a deficit. "You've got no future in basketball," he plausibly warned me. I ignored him.

To be sure, I always had athletic gifts. My earliest athletic memory is of grade school, probably the third grade or so, when the sides chosen at recess each day, in whatever the sport of the moment, would be Tony Atkiss, Jimmy Blackburn, and me against all the other boys in the class—the three best athletes against everyone else. This resulted, predictably, in outrageously one-sided games, since, notwithstanding the other team's superior numbers, we three little athletic princes would totally dominate the games. I'm always reminded of this when I hear the chatter—among adults!—about how "winning isn't everything, it's the only thing." For that was precisely the third-grade mentality we brought to those games. We were picking sides so as to assure that we would win by the largest score possible, and the absurd lopsidedness of those scores—things like "66-0"—didn't seem to bother us; in fact, it was the source of our pride. It also probably contributed to the premature end to an interest in sports for many of the other boys in the class. Within a year or two, however, we matured out of such absurdities and began to see that the real appeal of the game—any game—was to make its outcome precarious, to choose sides evenly so that the end would be genuinely open to question and that our chance of winning depended on our playing our very best and hustling the most. That was where the real fun was. Winning mattered, make no mistake about it, and we exhausted ourselves every day in the effort; but it wasn't everything. Years later, I would watch with delight as the same recognition dawned on my own two sons as they progressed through grade school. I've never forgotten that crucial lesson of the best sport: the appeal of precariousness, of risk taking, to human being, the desire to leave things—at least some things—genuinely open to question and a consequence of who can achieve their very best on a given occasion. Something in every athlete *wants* a large question mark at the beginning of every game, a question which is at once a challenge: who can play their best today? Only much later would I hear asserted as insight the simplistic principle of athletic competition that we had outgrown by fourth grade, that winning is the whole reason for playing.

Even as a child, then, I was among the athletically gifted and talented. I was always extremely quick and agile. I also hustled more than almost anyone else. Was that highly competitive quality also a natural gift, or was it somehow developed early on, in ways I cannot remember? Some of both, no doubt, but I confess I'm inclined more to the former. My parents were always interested in sports and encouraged my brother and me to participate.

But they certainly were not fanatical about it, in the manner of some accounts I've read of other parents with athletic children. I was surely not driven or programmed into sports by fanatic parents. I chose it because I loved it.

At most, however, these qualities—quickness, agility, competitiveness—might help explain my interest in athletics, not my specific choice of basketball as my sport. Part of it, probably, was that in those days basketball was the sport of sports in Philadelphia, where I grew up. It's also possible, of course, that in part I was overcompensating for my small stature by playing a "big man's" sport. If so, it was entirely unconscious, itself an implausible hypothesis for an elementary school youngster who didn't even know yet that basketball *was* a big man's sport. In any case, by the time I was in seventh grade and eligible to play on my first inter-scholastic team (the Junior High Team), my commitment was virtually total. In the locker room before our first game that year, I threw up from nervousness. It was the last time that ever happened. I also won the game with two foul shots in the final seconds. I was on my way.

For the next nine years or so, through high school and college, basketball was the center of my life, with all other commitments occupying various places on the periphery. With the exception of perhaps four or five days a year, my like-minded friends and I played basketball for several hours every day throughout the year. For us, the official season of basketball meant only that our games switched from the playgrounds to the more formal domain of team practice and games. But one way or another, we always played. In good weather, especially in the summer, we'd travel around the area from playground to playground, playing all day. Different courts had different "personalities," and we learned to adjust to each one. A court called "Aronomink" was habituated by the likes of Paul Arazin and Neil Johnston, players on the then Philadelphia Warriors of the NBA. It was hard to get in a game there, but you could learn a lot if you did. In Chester, Horace Walker and "Chubby" Foster, both college stars and both black, dominated the courts. At my "home court" at Lansdowne High, two of the other "name" guards who played there regularly were

Jim Lynam, who later played at St. Joseph's and then on to a coaching career with the Philadelphia 76ers and Baltimore Bullets, and Paul Westhead, who played at Lasalle and then had a coaching career that included tenures with the Los Angeles Lakers, Denver Nuggets, and various college teams. (No one who played with Paul in those days could be surprised at the "run and gun" game that has been his signature style as a coach!).

Needless to say, not all my encounters in those city-wide basketball travels were friendly; I certainly lived through my share of confrontations, arguments, and even occasions when things got so alienated that fights broke out and we had to run for our safety. But that, too, was instructive. The French writer and philosopher, Albert Camus, supposedly once said, reminiscing about his youth, "Then there were sports, from which I learned all that I know about ethics." Presumably an exaggeration from this active leader in the French underground, but perhaps also an exaggeration of a truth. In our everyday lives, where speech is the primary vehicle of our ethical encounters, it is notoriously easy to dissimulate. Much harder in sport, where the almost exclusive locus of ethical decision is physical action which is usually quite literally visible. In sport, we actually *see* what kind of ethical person you are: a cheat or a fair player, a coward or a malicious bully, a "whiner" or one who doesn't complain, a player who "gets away with anything he can" or a person of a higher ethical standard.

Other lessons were also available. On those courts, especially the ones in Chester or within the city proper, I began to have my first experiences of the absurdity of racism. Within the game itself, race usually was not an issue. The measure of a man was his jump shot. To keep on playing, you had to win. When picking sides, therefore, you picked the best player available, without regard to race. If you maintained the racial purity of your team at the price of picking the best player available, you paid a clear price for your racism. You'd lose, and, on the crowded courts of Philadelphia, it would sometimes be hours before you could get in another game. At a time when it would never have occurred to me to bring one of my black fellow players home to my house (nor they bring me to theirs), we nevertheless shared the kinship of the game. Gradually, the absurdity of that diremption began to come home to me.

It was at those thousands upon thousands of playground games, as well, that I learned one of the most important life lessons sport offers, a lesson that contradicts a teaching of many misguided coaches. No player, no matter how good, wins all his or her games in those playground encounters. Precisely because we do choose sides evenly to make it a good game, things tend to balance out over time. One learns to love winning, to be sure; that's the way you stay on the court for the next game. But you also learn to lose, not happily, but with the recognition that the sun still rises the next day after a loss, that there will be another game in an hour or so, or at the court across town, that defeat, however painful, is momentary, not necessarily enduring, and certainly not catastrophic. Some coaches try to persuade their players that life is not worth living after a loss, or that you cannot lose and keep your integrity as an athlete. No athlete who plays myriads of playground games can ever truly believe that.

In the winter, in bad weather, we'd drive around Philadelphia to the various college and prep school gymnasiums, sneaking into one, playing until a janitor found us and kicked us out, then moving on to the next. We played each individual game to win, that's for sure, and the intensity of the competition was sometimes fierce. But in the long run, we played to play. It was the appeal of the play, not some hysterical drive to win or dominate others, that brought us again and again to whatever court we could find our way into. Commentators on the sporting scene, especially its critics, fail to pay sufficient heed to this. All the psycho-babble about violent young males seeking an outlet for their aggression misses the enduring and surely ultimate reason why I and my friends played and played and played some more: the sheer fun of it, the joyful exuberance of running and jumping and banging into each other. One of the discoveries every good athlete makes somewhere along the way is that playing the game is more fun when you try hard to win, and the most fun of all when you out-hustle everyone else. Of course winning is important; it formally defines the end of every game, and athletes who invest the whole of their psychic and physical energy in a game are bound to be disappointed if they lose, even in a pick-up game. But the originary and enduring reason why athletes try so hard to win is their knowledge that that's the way to have the most fun. And the fun I've had over the years in the literally thousands of pick-up and formal basketball games I've played is hardly diminished by the recognition that my life-long won-lost record, like everyone else's, is probably pretty close to even.

All this practice produced its natural fruits. I became a very good basketball player. In high school, under the guidance of an outstanding coach who taught us the fundamentals of the game and who prided himself less on our wins than on how many of us went on to play college basketball, I became the star of our team, made the all-county team and played on a number of all-star teams throughout the city and its environs. In my senior year, my brother Artie was a sophomore, and the two of us gained considerable notoriety as a back court duo. Eventually, Artie would become a far better player than me, but at that time I was still the star. I began to assume that I'd go on to play in college. "There's always room on a team for a good little man," I was told countless times in apparent encouragement. I believed it.

Fortunately, my parents were strongly committed to education. The standing rule in our house was that my younger brother and I had to stay on the Honor Role if we wanted to keep on playing basketball. That, and certainly not any inherent enthusiasm for my studies, assured that I did very well academically, not that this was any great challenge. I am embarrassed to recall that when we had difficult English reading assignments in the "classics," (*Silas Marner, Great Expectations, Romeo and Juliet*, and the other usual high school suspects), I would purchase the respective "Classic Comic," read it, and usually do very well. Nevertheless, the upshot of this academic "pressure" from my parents was that I made National Honor Society, so my choice of colleges would not be limited by academic eligibility.

Perhaps because of my size, the really big-time basketball schools did not recruit me. But Princeton University did, and in the fall of 1957, I went off to Princeton to begin my college basketball career, and, quite incidentally to me at the time, my real education.

At Princeton, two defining changes occurred. First, a few superb teachers began to show me that something at once exciting and very important was happening in the pages of books. For the first time, I began to take my studies seriously for their own intrinsic interest and stake, not for some external reward or avoidance of punishment. That change eventuated in my choosing a career as a teacher and philosopher. One thing that did *not* happen, however, is that any of my teachers ever suggested to me that my intense involvement in basketball ought itself to be made an object of my reflection and my education.

Second, in my basketball playing I began the gradual transition from being a star to being just one of the players on the team. Fortunately, given the wonderful "chemistry" of the players on that team, the transition proved much less painful than it might have been. In any case, that, coupled with my growing interest in my studies, meant that basketball took a more rational place in my cosmos, though that place was still near the center. In those days, freshmen were ineligible for varsity competition; we had our own team, and a very good one it was. In a couple of years, we would become the core of a series of Ivy League championship teams. In our freshman year we improved our skills, got to know each other, formed close friendships, and had wonderful fun together. At the end of the season, I was honored by my teammates who elected me captain.

In my sophomore year, I was one of only two sophomores to earn a varsity letter. The team was dominated by four seniors, and it was an outstanding team indeed. We tied with Dartmouth for the Ivy Championship, then lost the play-off game by one point, literally in the final second. Presumably because the game was so close and both teams so good, the NCAA took the nearly unprecedented step of inviting two Ivy League teams into their tournament. But to our shock and outrage, the Athletic Director at Princeton ruled that no Princeton team that did not win the championship outright would be allowed to play in post-season play and declined the invitation. I always felt especially badly for the seniors, for whom this would have been their only chance to play in the tournament.

My position on the team that year proved important for the changes that were to come. On the one hand, I had to accept the fact that, virtually for the first time in my basketball career, I was not a star, indeed, not even a starter. On the other hand, I was one of only two sophomores to letter on a senior-dominated team. That, I think, enabled me to come to terms with the idea of being a subordinate contributor to a team while retaining my full self-confidence as a good player. I discovered that it could still be an experience powerful, rewarding, and fun.

In my junior year, my class more or less took over the team. One senior, Jim Brangan, a close friend from my hometown who had preceded me to Princeton, was the captain and star of the team. But we juniors comprised most of the rest of the team. We began to develop a closeness that was deep and rewarding. Three of the players were by now my roommates. We were all in the same "eating club" (Princeton's version of fraternities). For those who have not played on a high-level, high-intensity team, it would be hard to imagine just how much time a team spends together, how much our self-identities become bound up together. Basketball is a consummate team sport. The success of the team very much depends not simply on the individual talents of each of the players, but on how they succeed in meshing their skills. That meshing goes deeper than one thinks. It cannot be simply left behind when one leaves the court. To a considerable extent, our personalities, our very self-identities, also meshed. Who we were as a team was of course tied up with each other. But so, we learned, was who we were as individuals. We lived together, ate together, partied together, went out on dates together after games. It is a well-known cliche that men, by comparison to women, have difficulty expressing their emotions to each other. Perhaps because of the overtly shared passion of our commitment to the team and the emotions we expressed daily to each other in the heat of practices and games, we largely overcame that acculturated reticence. Very few things in our lives, in fact, were not shared. Our team was fortunate to be able to form a miniature community of kindred souls and deep friendships. As coaches like to point out, the fact that we were very good didn't hurt either.

Not that our little community was without its conflicts. One player, a sophomore destined to become an all-star and win the Ivy League scoring championship the following year, was the source of early tension. Not to put too fine a point on it, this player loved to score, and many of us had the distinct impression that the number of points he scored was at least as important to him as whether we won or not. There were some early confrontations, and many a discussion among us about how to deal with the problem. And those discussions bore fruit. Although there would occasionally for the next two years be some tension over his tendency to shoot too much, we never allowed it to undercut our efforts as a team, nor the fun we had. I mention this to underscore that this was no idyllic sports experience without tribulation, but one in which the depth of our friendship and love of the game overcame any obstacles that stood in our way.

Early in the season that year we played Temple in one of our pre-league games (Our wise old coach, "Cappy" Cappon, used to regularly schedule us against nationally ranked opponents in the early season before league play began. We would then show up for the Ivy League games with a poor record, but accustomed to a level of play which few of our Ivy opponents could match). I had been disappointed at the start of the season when I did not move immediately into a starting position on the team. I began the season still as the "sixth man." In the Temple game, I nevertheless played very well, scoring points and running the offense, as well as doing a pretty good defensive job on Temple's guard, "Pickles" Kennedy, who was an All-American candidate. The next day before practice, I decided it was time to confront the coach about starting. He observed that one of our limitations as a team

45

was that we were not especially big, and that that limitation was accentuated dramatically when I was in the lineup. He felt that he could not risk my being the "regular" guard at my height, fearing that other teams would take too much advantage of the height differential. I'd have to be satisfied with being a leading bench player. He may have been right, though I certainly didn't agree with him. One of the problems every top-level coach must face is that the leading substitutes on a team, by virtue of being the competitive athletes that they are, are almost certainly going to believe that they should start, and I was no exception. Under some circumstances, I might have been distraught or resentful. But here I was, on a very good team, with the best friends I had ever had, playing together day after day and doing very well. Under those circumstances, it would take a small soul indeed to retain a grudge. I found myself in an ambivalent position; I accepted my place on the team as once again a subordinate contributor, while disagreeing with the coach's decision to give me that place. I certainly thought I should be a starter. But with these friendships and this team, things were getting more complex; my individual athletic ego was hurt, but I was experiencing the rewards and satisfactions of an intense and positive involvement with a group that enabled me to subordinate, at least to an extent, my personal ambitions. Were I on a different team without the good chemistry and the deep friendships, I doubt very much if I would have dealt with the situation as equitably as I did on this team.

Because we had only one starter returning from the previous year's fine team, we were not highly regarded in the pre-season prognostications, even within the Ivy League. And truth to tell, many of the teams we played—and beat—were physically more athletic than us. We were a small team even for the Ivy League, as my coach had reminded me when I confronted him. But we began to learn how to play together extremely well and developed perhaps a more than warranted self-confidence as a team. We also enjoyed each other's company immensely. Once we got into our Ivy League games, we began to win again and again, and to the surprise of everyone but ourselves, we won the league championship outright.

It was in that year that I think I began really to understand the game of basketball, to have a sense of what was actually happening when the game is played well by a team. Basketball is one of those games, like soccer or lacrosse, in which the establishing of a certain rhythm and flow is crucial. That is why, parenthetically, people rightly object so much to the recent custom of calling one timeout after another in the final few minutes of a contest; it interrupts the flow so definitive of the game. It's also why one so often hears basketball coaches—but almost never baseball and only rarely football coaches—speak of "determining the pace" of the game. That flow has to do with five people moving in certain patterns established over long practice, patterns with variations that the players choose according to the call of the moment and how the opposing team is defending them. The oft-cited affinity of basketball and improvisational jazz has its source here; in both, a certain pattern or "theme" is established, then the players improvise out of that pattern according to what is called for by the action of the game. This is deeply an experience of anticipation and of knowledge that goes far beyond what any player or coach could adequately articulate. Nevertheless, let me try with one isolated case.

To this day, several coaches and generations after I played, the signature play of Princeton's basketball team is the so-called back-door play. The play is a consummate act of teamwork and sport psychology. It must be set up by engaging in a pattern of movement that invites the opposing team (or as we used to say, "suckers them") to begin "overplaying" on defense, staying very close to their man and perhaps trying to anticipate a pass so that they can make a steal. Once we see that an opposing player is beginning to overplay his man, I might start dribbling toward that teammate, while he made movements suggesting that he was coming toward the ball to receive a pass. I would then fake a pass to him. If we did it right, my exaggerated fake pass would make the opposing player have his weight forward in anticipation of challenging his man once he gets the ball (in the delicious cases, he'll actually be charging forward to intercept the pass), and my teammate will cut *behind* the defensive man (hence the term "back-door"), toward the basket. As he comes out from behind his opponent, I will throw him, about ninety percent of the time, a bounce pass which, when it works, he'll pick up and score an easy lay-up. Why a bounce pass? My teammate will be running at full speed and receive the pass just as he breaks out from behind the man guarding him; that is, he'll be catching the pass almost blind, and will therefore need a soft pass, which a bounce pass is. Moreover, if I threw a chest pass (so named because it is thrown and should be received chest high), the chances are better that my opponent will be able to reach out and deflect the pass. The bounce pass I throw will hit the floor almost at the defensive player's feet and will therefore be much harder for him to stop.

Now all this has taken several minutes to describe. A player in a game must "see" in a second whether the moment is ripe for the play: whether the defenseman is unweighted, whether his teammate sees the same thing, whether the path to the basket is clear. None of this can be thought through serially and as it were analytically. We use inadequate metaphors like "seeing" or "feeling" in a vain attempt to capture the kind of awareness and knowledge at work here. And this sort of process goes on not in isolated segments such as I just described but constantly within the rhythm of the game. Only after living through that pattern, that specific flow, again and again does one gradually learn not only what alternatives *can* happen in a given situation, but learn to anticipate which are *likely* to happen, an anticipation that comes only with a thorough knowledge both of the offensive pattern itself and of the individual players and their preferences, strengths, and weaknesses. The apparently magical "sense" that fine players develop of where people are, of what is possible, likely, and best in a given situation, is really not magical at all but an unarticulated knowledge, a kind of attunement to the flow of the game, to patterns, to people, and to the possibilities generated by their convergence. We learned to do that that year, and I learned as well never to limit my sense of knowledge to what can be explicitly articulated.

Princeton's coach at the time was Frank ("Cappy") Cappon, a man who had built an enviable record and reputation as a canny coach and strategist. He was nearing the end of his career and, we were to learn sadly the next year, of his life. Cappy was a fine coach, but certainly an anomaly at Princeton. At this bastion of conservatism and elitist good manners, Cappy had a vocabulary that would make the proverbial sailor blush, and he was not the least shy about using that vocabulary in very public situations. I remember one occasion when he used it on me, to the hilarity of everyone present. This occurred near the end of a home game—I think it might have been against Cornell—when we had a comfortable lead and were cruising easily in the final minutes to a victory. Our man-to-man offense that year was a flowing one which began with no pivot man. At the appropriate time, one of several designated big men could break into the pivot from the corner, a pass would go into him, everyone would begin cutting and all hell would break loose—at least that was the way it was supposed to work, and often enough did. Although in principle anyone could have broken into the pivot from the corner, it was an explicit understanding that only the biggest players on the team should take that position, for obvious reasons. Well, here we were, far ahead in the waning minutes of the game, so I, never without self-confidence or a sense of the absurd, broke into the pivot position reserved only for big men. Even before anyone could (or would!) throw me a pass, Cappy was off the bench and, in front of a crowd quieted by the obvious outcome of the game, yelled at the top of his lungs, "You little shit, get out of there!" Such, to the vast enjoyment of the home crowd, was the beginning and end of my career as a pivot man.

Our championship season was capped by its expected reward, a bid to the NCAA tournament. As always, the Ivy champions were seeded very low in the rankings, and we were paired in the first game against a very highly seeded team, Duke University. In what was for us an exciting occasion at Madison Square Garden in New York City, we were soundly beaten by Duke, and our glorious season was over. In a day or two, we were back at the gym playing basketball again.

In our senior year, unlike the previous season, we had almost the whole team coming back and were expected to do very well. We had lost our captain, Jim Brangan, but there was a rising sophomore who had broken the freshman scoring record and who was expected to be of great help: Art Hyland, my younger brother. Art was a great athlete, destined to become an All-Ivy League basketball player and an All-American lacrosse player. Most of us on the team, myself included, knew that in truth he was already better than me, and would probably beat me out for a starting position. My career at Princeton was in all probability going to include three varsity years as the "sixth man." And because of my brother! Still, everyone was taken aback on the first day of practice when Cappy immediately put Artie on the starting team, me on the second. Artie didn't even have to "beat me out." Again, this caused a curious situation. Everyone knew in their heart of hearts that Art would be the eventual starter. After all, we had been playing together informally all fall, and Art's ability had already shown itself clearly. But everyone also anticipated that he would have to demonstrate that superiority in practice, that I, as the rising senior, would get the first shot at the position vacated by Jim Brangan. But Cappy didn't have time for such rituals. He had to get ready for the first game, and he knew, as we did, who the starters would be.

This could have been trouble. After that first practice, I was hurt, Artie felt terrible, other players, especially my three roommates, felt that I had been "screwed." Once again I confronted Cappy before the next practice. He explained to me what in any case I already knew, that Artie was bigger and better than me, that he was going to start, and that Cappy didn't have time to indulge in placating hurt feelings and expectations. We had a season for which we had to prepare.

For reasons that I have never entirely understood, that settled the issue, and it was never much of a problem thereafter. What I don't fully understand is how I, such a competitive and at that time athletically ambitious person was able to accept this blow to my aspirations with an anger and indignation that essentially ended after a day. Perhaps it was in part that I knew Cappy was right. Unlike the previous season, I didn't really think I should start ahead of Artie, and the team would be much too small with both of us in there at once. Perhaps it was also that the guy who beat me out was my brother, with whom I was very, very close. Surely a factor was that I was surrounded on the team by close friends, including my brother. Finally, there was the sustaining expectation that, hell, we were about to have a great season and a great time. The upshot, in any case, was that I accepted what in the abstract should have been a huge blow to my athletic ego (which at the time was still most of my ego) without rancor. We got on with the season at hand.

And a memorable season it was. We even did fairly well in the pre-Ivy league games, beating the likes of Temple, Rutgers, and the University of Connecticut. Once the league season began, we more or less cruised to our second straight Ivy League Championship. We were extremely close as a team. Several of us had been roommates as well as teammates for three years. My brother was on the team. We were mostly, as by now the custom, in the same eating club. The kinship of the game spilled over inevitably into our lives, and we were vouchsafed a set of friendships that, in curious ways, the years have never withered, even though we rarely see each other today.

I'm reminded of the uncanny depth of friendship that intense experiences such as this can engender when, occasionally, I return to Princeton for a class reunion. It's barely an exaggeration to say that it's really a *team* reunion, for we former teammates spend much of our time together. We may not have seen each other for five, even ten years. Yet within a few minutes of our greeting each other, some long and deep set of memories and understandings kick in, and it's as if we have barely been apart. When I return from those reunions, I'm often astonished but delighted to say to myself, "I still like these guys; we understand each other."

But that senior season too was not without its trials. In the middle of the season, Cappy, our coach, suffered a severe heart attack (he would die later in the year). The assistant coach, "Jake" McCandless, who would later become Princeton's head football coach, took over for the rest of the season. Jake was a "football man" who, as was customary in those days, assisted other sports in other seasons. While he was no doubt very knowledgeable in football, probably most of the players on our team knew more about basketball than he did. We won the championship largely by remembering what Cappy had taught us. But that was not the major problem with the coaching transition.

Cappy was an anomaly in those days in another way. He gave us no training rules. None. In my sophomore year, after the first practice and expecting, as had always happened in the past, to have an elaborate set of training rules presented to us, from curfew hours to diet, I was surprised to hear nothing on the subject from Cappy. I was so surprised, in fact, that after practice I asked him what the training rules were. I've always remembered his reply: "Live so that you can go full speed the whole game." We were supposed to be adults, and Cappy treated us as adults. In our case, his strategy worked perfectly. We would usually have a beer or two after a game, but we really did take care of ourselves on our own. Other teams with whom we had occasion to talk were shocked on two grounds, that Cappy gave us such freedom, and that we didn't abuse it.

Jake McCandless, however, had other ideas. He had come to Princeton from a coaching position at a prep school, and he brought with him a number of prep school attitudes. Immediately upon taking over the team, in the middle of a season in which we were leading the Ivy League, and with a team accustomed to having the coach treat us as adults, he imposed a stringent set of training regulations on us, including bedtime hours on the road trips and a complete ban on alcohol. We responded by making a game of breaking all his rules. I remember one hilarious evening on a road trip when one of our players, who in fact never drank anyway, made an exception in this case, went with us to some sort of Polynesian bar, bought one of those elaborate drinks with a gardenia floating on top, drank it, then left the glass and wilted gardenia outside the coach's hotel room with a note to the effect that the phantom was striking again, or some such thing. Once again, our team exhibited the peculiar ability to respond positively to a potentially damaging psychological situation. Instead of merely being resentful of Jake's rules, we added to our fun by breaking them.

Nor was that the end of our difficulties. As I've said, we won the Ivy League Championship for the second year outright. Our first NCAA tournament game, again in Madison Square Garden, was against George Washington University, winner of the Southern Conference, much bigger than us and heavily favored. Several minutes into that game, Don Swan, our captain, one of my roommates, and my close friend, had his legs cut out from under him and fell on his head. The floor at Madison Square Garden at that time was a foldout floor that could be taken up and put back to make room for ice hockey games. It had large cracks at the joints, and unfortunately, Don's head landed on one of those cracks. It split his head and severed an artery as well. As it turned out, Don's injuries were limited to some stitches and a severe concussion. But at the moment, we were afraid he was dying, as blood spurted from the artery in his head in huge jets and he went into convulsions. We were all utterly terrified. After Don was taken to the hospital and the floor cleaned of his blood, there ensued one of those curious phenomena of athletic psychology. Having lost our captain and star forward, one would have expected us to be in even worse straits than most considered us in from the beginning. But exactly the opposite happened. Were we somehow inspired and did we overcompensate for the loss of our captain and friend? Did the George Washington players suffer an unconscious guilt because of his injury? Whatever the case, to the surprise of everyone, we won the game by a whopping 17 points. For the first time in twenty years, an Ivy League team would advance beyond the first game in an NCAA tournament, and they were us.

So we went to Charlotte, North Carolina for the Eastern Quarterfinals (now popularly called the "Sweet Sixteen") without our captain and without our coach. We were, needless to say, decided underdogs against St. Joseph's, a big, talented, top-ten team with designs on the national championship. The betting line listed us as twelve-point underdogs. On the other hand, we surely had nothing to lose, and, as we discovered upon entering the Coliseum for warmups, it was practically like a home game. The fans were almost entirely on our side, possibly because we were such underdogs, more probably because St. Joseph's was a Catholic college, and we were deep in the Protestant Bible Belt. The game went pretty much as anticipated, with St. Joseph's gradually pulling away until, with about four minutes to go, they had a twelve-point lead, just as the betting line had predicted. At that moment, my brother fouled out on a controversial call, and I went in to take his place.

Sport psychologists call it a "peak experience." It's an occasion when, somehow, one's immersion in the game is total, and all of one's skills built up laboriously over the years magically come together so that one plays at one's absolute peak, though seemingly effortlessly. I entered the game, probably, as I reflected while reporting to the scorer's table, to be my last game for Princeton. The next four minutes are as a moment. I was so totally "in" the game that the actual sequence of events is now a blur, though I recall vividly most of the discrete events themselves. But I know this; the Zen gurus who speak of "becoming one with the game" have a point. All the activity of my mind, indistinguishable now from the activity of my body, became involved in, yet determinative of, the rhythm and flow of the game. I became part of it in a way that is not adequately expressed by saying that *I* was a participant *in* the game. Such language draws too arbitrary a dichotomy between my own activity and the game, as if I and the game were discrete entities. It would be closer to the truth to say that I *became* the game—though of course, not I alone. I remember that we began to catch up, that we stole the ball again and again, scoring each time, so that the pandemonium of the spectators made more forceful still the excitement of knowing that we were catching up. I stole the ball twice, scored both times, told myself to keep hustling. We kept coming on, driven by the intensity of the game itself, intensified still further by the indefinite but pervasive roar of the crowd. As St. Joseph's was coming down the court I ran to deflect a pass, batted it into the air and ran to grab it. I turned to throw the ball to a teammate alone on his way for an easy score when the referee's whistle blew. When I had hit the ball into the air and run to retrieve it, he called me for an "air dribble." The crowd erupted in protest. I looked at the scoreboard for the first time since I had entered the game. There were ten seconds left. We were losing by one point, one point which, if the referee had not blown his whistle, would have been our margin of victory instead of defeat.

It was not really sadness that pervaded the locker room as we sat there, mostly glancing at each other and back at the floor. Nor was it depression, anger, bitterness. There was something simple, a oneness among us all, which both signaled a termination yet would always be; a silent calmness that bespoke a deep realization; something had come to an end.

And that end had at least two senses, end in the sense of finality, that a certain kind of peculiarly intense experience, that of playing on a Division I athletic team, was no longer to be, but also end in the sense of completion, an experience brought to fulfillment, an intimation of completeness. It has always seemed to me that athletics offers something which, on the aesthetic level, all great art offers, and which may be one of the ultimate sources of appeal to human being of both art and athletics: a suggestion of a completed theme in a life characterized by the most radical and decisive partiality. It could be said that our day to day lives are shot through with incompleteness—jobs left undone, aspirations unfulfilled, human frustrations everywhere. In the midst of this partiality, athletics, by the very fact that games have time limits, impose a momentary if arbitrary possibility of completeness, a theme of life begun and brought to fulfillment. This completeness, even if arbitrary, discloses to us something of the satisfaction of completeness which we all seek again and again, a seeking which Plato characterized as our eros and regarded as virtually definitive of the human condition.

This intimation of completeness is revealed as well in another dimension of my athletic experience, what I referred to in my account of my last game as the phenomenon of immersion. What is there about the intensity of an athletic game that allows us, at least for the moment, to "forget" all of our other involvements, to invest our entire being, body and soul, in this project which will have next to no effect on the world? And why is that totality of immersion so satisfying, so appealing to those of us who have once tasted of its fruits? Perhaps Plato is right after all. There is a drive in us for a transcendence of the fragmentation which is our daily lot, for a completeness rarely if ever attainable in a whole life. In their finality, however arbitrary, and in the totality of immersion that they invite, athletic games give us an intimation of that transcendence, our first sense, perhaps, of what genuine wholeness would be like.

But the other side of that intimation, and always present in sport, is finitude. My last game at Princeton brought home to me that finitude with dramatic force, but it is always present in one way or another in sport. We learn in athletic games that the end of a game, or a season, or an athletic career, is at once limitation and what grants the possibility of meaning. The end limits us, to be sure, and in an obvious and often frustrating sense. "If only we had had another minute," someone might have said about our comeback against St. Joseph's, but the rules of the game say that we did not. Yet without that limit of the arbitrary end, what meaning would the game have? Games that go on forever, or in which we forget the score and forget that the game will have an end when someone will win or lose, are not more but less meaningful, liberal wishful thinking notwithstanding. How uncanny it is that the clearly defined, arbitrary end of the game at once places a decisive limit on our possibility yet grants to our activity the meaning it has. And what of the finitude of our lives?

The finitude of which I have spoken so far is a dimension of the temporality of the game, but that temporality has a richness that exceeds the simple fact that the game (season, career, life) ends. I know of no experience that has brought home as forcefully to me the power of the phenomenological account of "lived time," than my basketball experience. Our experience of temporality is not one of discrete, atomistic, and exactly measurably moments (seconds, minutes, etc.) but something richer, more alive, more flowing. What better demonstration could there be than the intense, focused temporality of a basketball game, of the experience of time as a convergence in the moment, or rather a constant reconvergence, of the "past"—what has been in the game so far—and the "future"—our projects or intentions of what is to happen—into the "present"—the activity I am performing now?

A short coda must be added. The day after our loss to St. Joseph's, the newspaper accounts of our exciting comeback and the controversial referee's call at the end the game were overshadowed by other, more ominous sports news. News of the infamous basketball point-shaving scandal of 1961 had broken, and the papers were full of it. Even worse, three players on the St. Joseph's team to whom we had lost the night before had been indicted for point-shaving. We were crushed. Was our great comeback, in which we were already taking such pride, the result not of our own efforts but of sleazy point-shaving by the St. Joseph's players? To our enormous relief, the answer turned out to be no. Although the three St. Joseph's players had indeed shaved points during the regular season, they had agreed that, in their quest for a National Championship, they would not do so during the NCAA Tournament. Our comeback had been authentic, our pride restored.

So ended my formal career as a basketball player. Yet I've never stopped playing, even, to the occasional consternation of loved ones who care about my health, to this day. My skills diminish, sometimes seemingly daily, but I remain drawn irresistibly to the game. Over the years, I've taken up other sports as putative substitutes, sports more appropriate for no longer youthful legs and muscles. I tried running for a while, until Achilles tendinitis forced my retirement. I skied downhill until it got too expensive. I cross-country ski when it snows. A year or two ago I took up squash, which is great fun, and cycling. But when I hear there's a lunch time basketball game at the gym, I still can't stay away. As often as not, I come back from the game shaking my head disconsolately at the loss of my skills, wondering why pride in the memory of my former abilities doesn't insist that I retire. But every once in a while I'll throw just the right pass at exactly the right moment to the precise spot where my teammate ought to receive it; or I'll take a shot that feels exactly right and that I know as soon as it leaves my hands it's going in the basket, or in the midst of the intense action of the game I'll make a move "without thinking about it," calling it up from the depths of my body memory, and it will be exactly the right thing to do. Then I think to myself in heartfelt imitation of the old NBA television commercial, "I love this game."

Addendum

I'm now, in 2025, 86 years old. I stopped playing pick-up basketball when I was 62, some twenty years ago. "Out of respect for the game," I tell my friends, though the real reasons had more to do with the way the younger set (younger than me, anyway) seemed to me to be moving more and more towards the "run and gun" kind of basketball. I still loved the "run" part; it was the gunning that pissed me off more and more. Their attitude towards passing, it seemed to me, was that it was an admission of defeat: "I can't get off a shot, so what the hell, I'll pass it to someone else." Remembering a remark of the great Boston Celtic center, Bill Russell, on a TV show when he was asked when he would retire and he replied, "When it's no longer fun," I swallowed hard and hung up my basketball shoes.

But over twenty years later, I *still* can't get past the sense that I'm a basketball player. Despite a reasonably successful academic career, my sense of self-identity remains deeply tied to the fact that I played basketball. My diminishing ability to remember this or that is not the most irritating thing about growing old. It's that I can no longer jump! I used to say, before the COVID 19 pandemic seems to have ended my squash playing, that I could still run around the squash court. Now the best thing I can say is that I "hurry." I'm not sure what to say about this, except that it's testimony to the depth and power of my experience of basketball. For me, as I suspect for many former players, basketball was no "extra-curricular activity." It was, and in a strange way still is, who I am.

But, someone might say, at least you can still be a basketball *fan!* The truth is, not really. Unless I "have skin" in the game (the Princeton basketball team, my sons' games and now my grandchildren's), I'm not really a "fan." I do occasionally watch games on TV, but from an aesthetic standpoint. I want to see the game played well, and it doesn't matter much to me who wins. I usually end up coaching from my couch. "Back-door him!" "See the pass!" I suspect this is because almost my entire interest in basketball, indeed in sports generally, is in the *experience of playing*. Virtually all my writing on philosophy of sport has been from the standpoint of *playing* the game, not watching it. A friend of mine, Simon Critchley, has recently published a most interesting and lively book entitled *What We Think About When We Think About Football* (He's English, and he means what Americans call soccer). It is written almost entirely from the standpoint of the fan, and it is full of insights and striking observations. It struck me as I read the book that he could make a perfectly legitimate criticism of my work on sport that I have more or less ignored the sociologically important phenomenon of sports fandom. He speaks early on of his work being loosely "phenomenological," but it is largely the phenomenology, the showing forth, of what the fan sees and experiences. By contrast, almost my entire focus has been on the experience of the player, including, certainly, my own. So it is perhaps less surprising that I am not much of a basketball *fan*.

One more thing: recently on a national news program, I heard two black activists from Chicago interviewed about a recent spate of violence in Chicago. One was a minister, the other a well-known rapper. When asked, "What should we tell our minority youth about this violence," one of them replied: "Tell them the truth; they almost never hear the truth from public figures." That made me think back to the somewhat sunny account I gave of my traveling with my friends to the largely black playgrounds of Philadelphia and Chester, how I dismissed with a phrase the occasional times when animosity reigned, and characterized my experience as largely a positive and friendly one of engagement with the black players on their "home" courts. I wonder; did I "say the truth"? It was certainly *my* truth, the way I recall those experiences. But was it the truth of the experience of those black players with whom we played? Or was their experience tinged with a certain resentment, even bitterness, that they suppressed for a time? I don't and cannot know. But I'm struck by the contrast with an experience I had years later, when I was a young professor at Trinity and still playing basketball occasionally with the players on Trinity's men's basketball team. It was shortly after Martin Luther King's murder, and turmoil was abroad throughout the country, including in Hartford. In a well-meaning if naïve effort to show solidarity and sympathy with the black youth in the "north end" of Hartford, I gathered a few of the Trinity players, both black and white, and we went to one of the well-known courts in the north end, hoping to get in some games with the otherwise entirely black players there. We stood there for over an hour and were pointedly ignored as the successive games were played. We simply were not wanted. That was a much more explicit repudiation of us than anything I recall on the courts of Philadelphia. Times had changed, and not in a positive way.

CHAPTER 3

On Being Married to an Artist

"Walk in beauty!"

(Navajo farewell)

I might begin, frivolously, with the allergies, symbol in almost Proustian fashion of an artist's excessive sensibility, of the suffering that is the limit of an exceeding openness and responsiveness to one's environment. Anne and I sometimes joke that were she to go on the six o'clock news each evening and simply report the state of her sinuses, her weather predictions would be superior to the best of the professional meteorologists. But that is only a symbol, and indeed a frivolous one.

I don't remember when she became an artist in the self-identifying sense that names not just something that we do but who we are. When I met her, she was taking a course in pottery at Penn State University while majoring in something called "Liberal Studies," which allowed her to study pretty much whatever she wanted. That included all kinds of things, among which, as it happened, was a course in logic in the Philosophy Department, and an advanced course in gourmet cooking. As a somewhat impoverished graduate student at the time, I was the direct beneficiary of the leftovers in the latter course. In the logic course, Anne was tickled by what struck her as the absurd sterility of reducing to logical symbols phrases that carried real meaning as articulated language. One example from Irving Copi's *Introduction to Logic* always exemplified to her such absurdity: students were asked to formulate in logical symbols the proposition, "Apples and oranges are delicious and nutritious." Today, covering most of one wall in my office at Trinity College is a large ceramic mural, full of bright colors and sculpted and photographic images, set up in an elaborate grid whose visual and associational meanings are endlessly rich. Its title is "Apples and Oranges are Delicious and Nutritious." It is Anne's ever-present reminder to me of the difference between the richness of lived experience and the sterile abstractions to which philosophy can reduce the real if it misses its proper calling.

Was she already an artist then as a college student? When we got married and moved to Toronto where I had my first teaching position, she continued to take pottery courses at a local craft center. But that interest seemed of necessity something of a side light to the pressing tasks of giving birth to, then masterminding the raising of, our first son. Still, she was already taking offense when someone referred to pottery as her "hobby," and that might have told someone something.

When, after three years in Toronto, we moved to Hartford and I took a position at Trinity College, Anne became a member of Wesleyan Potters in Middletown, an organization that included both pottery classes and facilities for both amateur and professional potters to work, where she began taking courses much more regularly. All of a sudden, it seemed, she was doing shows, winning awards, selling her work, and before long, she was no longer a student at "the pottery" but a member of the teaching faculty. Also all of a sudden, or so it seemed, she did not just "do pottery;" she was an artist.

So for the last thirty years I have lived in the intimate presence of an artist without being one myself. That has meant living in the regular presence of a remarkable sensibility altogether different from my own, a difference about which I'm often moved, as now, to wonder, and to turn over in my mind. I grew up in a family of two sons, and as previous essays have indicated, both the children became so totally involved in sports that it would be no exaggeration to say that sports dominated our family life, and not just for my brother and me. Our parents, both very supportive of our athletic activities, spent enormous amounts of time going to our games, socializing with the other athletes' parents, taking us to games, and generally arranging their lives according to our athletic schedules. For most of my memory, our family life centered around sports.

Anne, on the other hand, was the middle of three sisters. Only much later, when she was in high school, was a son born into the family, but by that time Anne was almost ready to go off to college. So she, by contrast, grew up in a "female" house, and one whose concerns only tangentially involved sports. The contrast is striking; I grew up in a family whose central focus was the boys' involvement in sports. Anne grew up in a family of girls, whose focus involved so many other things that sports was entirely peripheral. Yes, she played high school field hockey and was a cheerleader, but, in accordance with the social norms of the day, not with anything like the passion that my brother and I invested in basketball.

As we formed our own family, it came about that we, too, had two sons, and in next to no time (thanks in part to my wildly enthusiastic encouragement) it was clear that they were both athletically gifted. A central focus of our family life soon became one with which I, but not Anne, was altogether familiar and comfortable: sports.

There were occasional, no doubt well-justified protests. But before long, Anne had developed another, entirely positive way of coming to terms with a trio of males hopelessly devoted to sport; she began to integrate her family's enthusiasm for sports and games into her artwork. There began to emerge from her hands a series of "game" pieces. Some were pieces on surfaces that imitated game boards and actually looked like board games—except that the "pieces" were little ceramic models of cars and planes reminiscent of the children's youthful toys. One game piece poked fun at my own philosophical encounter with the writings of Jacques Derrida. It was a piece with all sorts of small ceramic letters and absolutely no rules, that she called "Derry-da-da." It hangs today on the wall of my study. Shortly thereafter, she began to work with photographic images on clay, and this enabled her to integrate actual photo images of her family, often playing sports, into her work.

So began a process which has characterized her artwork as it has matured; the integration of her family life into the pieces she makes, part of a growing conviction on her part that art, her art at least, is inevitably personal. Needless to say, her work did not exclusively refer to her family; her experience, after all, was and is richer than the limits of her family. But that her family life was a powerful experience to which she wanted to respond, that was evident in her work. After the game pieces came a series of pieces that included photographic and molded images of her family (and occasionally the body parts thereof!). The piece on my office wall, "Apples and Oranges Are Delicious and Nutritious," is a culminating example of that. More recently, she has begun making large ceramic mosaic pieces that sometimes include digitized images of the family as part of the work. One is a self-portrait, another a piece that includes childhood images of our younger son and his cousin, entitled "Boyos Boyos." Her most recent version of this is a monumental mosaic piece that dominates the vestibule of the new gymnasium at Western Connecticut State University, containing digitized images of athletes, of whom one of the basketball players is me.

So what I am at long last trying to do in these essays, to thematize explicitly aspects of my personal life into my work as a philosophic writer, is something that Anne has been doing in her art work for years. If one agrees with Proust, this "remembrance" of one's life by lifting it up into a work of art constitutes the only justification of life itself, a literal affirmation of Nietzsche's famous remark that "Only as an aesthetic phenomenon can life be justified." In Anne's work, that desire to lift up aspects of one's life into art strikes me as altogether more positive. Not as the "only" way life can be justified, but as an affirmation of its richness, of its impact on her consciousness, she incorporates the visual images of her own life into a "yea-saying" of enduring beauty.

I do not want to hazard universal claims about "all art." But I wonder if at least often, the impetus to art arises from something like the source it seems to for Anne, a kind of "de trop" experience of life. For those of us sufficiently sensitive to it, sufficiently open to its power, life is "too much" to leave alone, to take it simply as it is. It can of course be too much in a negative as well as in a positive sense. Either way, such an experience of life demands a response. If, as in Anne's case, that response involves a preserving of the power of lived experience in a work of enduring beauty, that surely is an act of exhilarating affirmation. If one lives in the presence of such a person and the works that issue from her, one lives in a state of repeated avowal and challenge: avowal of the richness and power that life can carry, challenge to be as open and responsive to it. In one's own way.

But in Anne's case at least, the movement is not just unidirectional, from life experience into art. The art she makes also transforms our life into an enhanced aesthetic richness. This is nowhere so clear for me as in the case of our home, which in one sense is in the midst of becoming Anne's largest ongoing artwork. We bought the house, under rather curious conditions, some fifteen years ago. The house sits in a cluster with several others in a heavily wooded area along the Salmon River. Our land begins at the end of a short country road called "Town Farm Road," so named because it once was the location of the town poor farm, where indigents of the village, down on their luck and means, could live and earn their keep farming the land. The six houses in the little community are organized as a condominium; we each own our own houses, plus an undivided interest in the 90 acres or so of land, the south border of which is the Salmon River. On the east and west borders, small streams feeding down into the Salmon mark the boundaries of the Salmon River State Forest. The land immediately surrounding our house slopes downward toward the river. A field of several acres expanse extends from our house down toward a large stand of tall white pine, planted in neat rows years ago by the workers on the poor farm. A path through those pines takes us to the river, about a quarter of a mile away. Surrounding us on the other sides, woods. The setting is stunningly beautiful. The houses were another story. They were built about twenty years ago by an eccentric and, as we were to learn later, rather mean-spirited millionaire whose only known occupation, apparently, was to build houses for his own pet projects, of which this little community was the largest. Though we didn't know it at the time, he was a not-quite architect, never having completed his architectural training, and this showed in his work. The houses were starkly minimal ("simple building" was the spin he put on them), with exposed metal hinges for the posts and beams, corrugated metal ceilings, particle board for walls, no closet space and no cellar or attic for storage. We bought it in part because of the sheer beauty of the setting, in larger part because we felt an almost desperate need to move to a place with more space than we had at the small house in the conventional little neighborhood that we had bought ten years before, with no space available to build and fire a raku kiln, which Anne often employed at that time. And it was relatively cheap, so we thought we could afford it. Still, I was initially reluctant to buy into such stark rusticity. Our parents and other relatives, sometimes outspokenly, thought we were crazy. But the artist in the family saw possibilities where we only saw problems. So, whether foolishly or insightfully, we bought the house, and Anne soon set to work on her most ongoing art project, the transformation of our house from an aesthetic abomination into an aesthetic affirmation, one that would not insult but deserve to belong in the beauty of its surroundings.

The transformation began with the obvious: cover the metal ceilings, cover or paint the particle board walls, build some storage space. The walls were adorned with Anne's artwork and the work of some of our artist friends. But before long, transformations of a much more radical sort began to take place. The most striking early one is the kitchen, in which the drab particle board walls have been replaced by porcelain tiles of Anne's own making, containing strikingly colorful orange and red images of fruits and vegetables. The white tiles and bold colors brighten the kitchen.

The references to food affirm the activity that happens there so regularly. But the work as a whole intensifies that affirmation, at once says yes to it while suggesting that it is an activity of life and of family worth preserving, worth being presented not just as a daily activity but as an issue for reflection and thoughtfulness. Anne's next tile wall project is our bathroom.

It is deeply satisfying to live in a house of such enhanced aesthetic quality. But I'm moved as well by the thought-provoking way in which Anne at once affirms the power of her home life by transforming it into enduring art, while at the same time, by that very art, making of her home her own work of art. The wholeness of this circle is remarkable: an openness and responsiveness to the intensities of life generates her art, and that art, in turn, transforms and enhances the quality of her life and those vouchsafed to live with her. Socrates' most famous epithet is probably "the unexamined life is not worth living," a challenge to subsequent generations of philosophers that has all too rarely been met. Anne's artist version of the Socratic dictum, authentically lived, might well be, "the life untransformed into art is not worth preserving."

In recent years, Anne has moved this circle of transformation I described above outside the house to the gardens we have grown. Granted a good amount of open space, we have grown large gardens, both flower and vegetable gardens. I shall have more to say on my own experience of gardening in a subsequent essay. Here I note, first, that while Anne and I both work on the vegetable garden, with me bearing perhaps the brunt of the work there, Anne takes the lead in caring for the flower gardens. Now I know many men who are wildly enthusiastic about flower gardening, so I suspect this is not just a phenomenon of gender inscription. In our case, rather, it has more to do with a natural aesthetic authority that Anne has by virtue of being the artist that she is. Responsively open to her environment, to color, to composition, to beauty in ways beyond my ken, she includes the flower gardens in her aesthetic domain. She is now planning some outdoor ceramic sculptures that will at once articulate that natural beauty and more deeply join it to the artistic consciousness that lives in and through it. One of them is a piece inspired in part by a poet friend of ours, Carl Cesar, a simple phrase that says, "This is not just words, you know." He no doubt is referring to his poetry. By making a ceramic piece, perhaps ten feet long, composed of raku fired letters that spell out the phrase, she adds multiple senses to the original phrase. The piece itself, now in ceramic letters, is surely "not just words," and if one takes the "this" to refer to the surrounding garden in its beauty, we get yet another register of meaning to this remarkable piece, this remarkable artistic enhancement of our environment.

Often we take walks around the ninety acres or so that the little community here shares. I am not so much of an aesthetic oaf that I do not appreciate full well the beauty of the place. But Anne's aesthetic appreciation of the same space is of a different order. What tends to move me on our walks is the experience of familiarity in a place once so strange; that I now walk with the comfort of being at home on paths once known in the same way to native Americans of the Wangunk tribe. Or I often imagine what it would be like to gain the literal sustenance of one's life from this land, as the poor villagers did long ago who built the stone fences that cut here and there through our land, fences that once no doubt defined fields and boundaries, but which now serve only to invoke wonder in an occasional wanderer. What usually moves me, then, is my sense of participation in the history of the place, of my familiar immersion in this land once home to others. Typical, perhaps, of a philosopher. Anne's experience of the place strikes me as much more immediate and sensuous. She sometimes picks up items to bring home to photograph or draw or incorporate directly into her art: pieces of wood, or bird feathers, or, once, a huge, abandoned wasp nest. She notices striking colors or forms, of trees, plants, wildflowers, even the garishly bright colors of some molds, that she might incorporate into her work. In a way, her artistic consciousness accomplishes a wonderfully Hegelian gesture, taking what is out there as other, and literally incorporating it into her own life through art. It is an active, an immediate, and a powerful response to the experience of her life. But it's also just an extension, really, of what her art has always been. I live, then, conjoined to another who I know will always take that which is most powerful in our experience and transform it, elevate it, preserve it, in her own way, the way of art, and beauty.

Navajo culture, as I understand it, seems founded upon what spokesmen for European culture would call aesthetics. As the farewell that begins this essay suggests, the guiding theme of Navajo life seems to be to "walk in beauty," that is, first, to see the beauty in the coursing of the world, and then to get oneself into attunement, into harmony with that beauty. A famous example is the Navajo attitude toward occasional periods of drought. Whereas most indigenous tribes might respond to that situation with a rain dance, or some other effort to propitiate the divinities so that they will change the course of nature and bring rain, that is, make the course of nature consistent with human desires, the Navajo way is, first, to see the beauty in the way things are, and second, instead of asking that it be changed, to put oneself into harmony with that way, to "walk in beauty." A second example: the thing that is wrong, from the Navajo standpoint, with things like stealing or violence, is that it is ugly, out of harmony with nature, a failure to walk in beauty. One of the intriguing things about this view of things is that, again to speak in the language of western philosophy, it is a metaphysics of aesthetics, yet another thought-provoking version of the Nietzschean view that "only as an aesthetic phenomenon is life justifiable." To live with an artist is to live in the presence of someone who experiences the world and lives it out in something like the Navajo way. To be sure, Anne's art, her transformation of life into art, is not necessarily defined by the issue of beauty (though that is surely a central theme of her work and life) and her construal of beauty is certainly not confined to "harmony." Nevertheless, it shares with the Navajo way the notion that the appropriate response to the coursing of one's life is an aesthetic one, that one should best respond to it in and through art, and yes, that one should see the beauty in it.

Occasionally, I return to Penn State University, usually for some philosophic conference or other. When I do, I always take a walk to the steps of the library where, years ago, Anne and I were first introduced. It is a gesture, in part, of romance, but also, surely, one of thanksgiving.

Addendum

In the 90's of the twentieth century and the early years of the twenty-first, Anne became the artistic director of a small art gallery in Cambridge, Massachusetts. Particularly for the setting up of shows at the gallery and the "openings," this soon necessitated that we find a place in the Boston area for Anne to stay when business at the gallery called, and for me to join her on weekends. We began with a small pied-a-terre in Boston's North End of Boston. After a while, we expanded to a small but more substantial condominium in Somerville. When I went on "phased retirement" from Trinity College in 2010, we made the decision to sell our house in the woods of Connecticut, dubbed by our relatives "the rugged condo," and move to the much less rugged locale of a house in Somerville. Anne and I were both a bit surprised at ourselves because we felt relatively little nostalgia about leaving this home that had been so important to us in so many ways. But we began to realize as we got older that the "rugged condo" was becoming increasingly more rugged to us, especially when winter snowstorms occurred, or when we needed to get to certain things of the city faster than our 45—minute car trip to Hartford allowed. In addition to Anne's gallery work, another draw of the Boston area was that by then, both our now grown children and their families live close to Boston, Chris in Foxboro, Craig in Cambridge. So we moved to a house in Somerville. Happily, Anne was able to continue her artwork unabated. We set up a kiln and her potter's wheel in our sizable basement, and Anne soon joined a kind of artists' cooperative in an old factory building where several floors had been given over to artist's studios. So Anne was able to continue both to make her work and to show it in her gallery at "Vernon Street Studios" as it is known. Until about two years ago, when, as we knew was typical of ceramic artists getting on in years, her back began to give out. When, in March of 2020, we seized an opportunity to move next door to our son, Craig and his family in Cambridge, we decided to donate the pottery equipment to local studios and gave up Anne's gallery. So now, Anne, like me, is "retired." But happily, our enjoyment of her artwork lives on, with many of her pieces adorning our relatively new house in Cambridge. Retired she is, but I still feel that I live with an artist. And if you asked her, I'm sure she'd tell you she still is one.

CHAPTER 4

Fishing and Farming

I am trying to teach my mind
to bear the long, slow growth
of the fields, and to sing
of its passing while it waits.

(WENDELL BERRY)

I GREW UP IN Lansdowne, Pennsylvania, a town immediately on the border of west Philadelphia, and therefore a town in an uneasy vacillation between city and suburbia: not quite of the city, and with clear aspirations, especially in those days, to be suburban, but too close to the city, geographically and culturally, to be accepted as equal by the genuine suburban towns like those on the "main line" of Philadelphia, a large step up in social class and a few miles further from the city itself. Especially because of my intense involvement in basketball, my own orientation leaned very much toward the city, where the best basketball was, where the big games were, where the athletic action was.

Two utterly minor consequences of this orientation, at least at the time, were that my young life had nothing to do with fishing or with farming, two activities that, if asked in those days, I would have certainly associated with country "hicks." I have a vague recollection that once, probably before I was ten, my father dutifully decided that he should give my brother and me a fishing experience. On opening day of the fishing season, he took us to visit my uncle, who lived in farm country outside Lancaster, Pennsylvania, and we all went to fish at a stream my uncle knew, which proved to be a stream that apparently everyone else in the Lancaster area knew, since they were lined up several people deep along the stream. I doubt if we stayed more than an hour before my cousin, brother and I persuaded our fathers to go do something fun. That was my only recollection of a youthful fishing experience.

My farming experience was not even that rich. I'm told that during the war years (which means before I was six), my brother and I had a "victory garden" on a strip of undeveloped turf near our house in Lansdowne. But I'm only told of this; I have no memory of it whatsoever, nor of any other experience that had anything to do with growing things.

Yet as an adult and especially in recent years, two of the activities that have given me the most sustained if mellow pleasure have been fishing and farming, so much so that my home now is in the country, a good 25 mile commute from the college in Hartford, a place where I farm about an acre of land and where our land borders the Salmon river, one of the better fishing streams in the state. How and why should it, could it, come about that a city kid should end up living a life sustained in part by rural pleasures?

I remember well the beginnings of my enjoyment of fishing. I was in graduate school, and between my first and second years there I took a summer job as an athletic counselor and teacher at a "school-camp" for mostly maladjusted rich kids in Dexter, Maine, a small town in central Maine, perhaps a half hour or so south of Moosehead Lake. I returned to the camp for several summers, even after Anne and I were married, and during that time, got to know some of the local people who worked as carpenters and mechanics at the camp, men with such memorable names as Eben, Rufus, and Armand. For whatever the reasons, these men took a shine to me, and among the blessings they conferred was that they introduced me to fishing and camping in the Maine wilderness. They took obvious delight in helping this young "flat-lander" (the mildly condescending name by which native Mainers refer to all visitors from south of Maine) buy his first fishing pole and the other accoutrements I'd need for the trip they invited me on during one of my free weekends that first summer. They took even more delight in watching my uncomfortable reaction to my first night sleeping under the stars in the wilderness of northern Maine, above Moosehead Lake, where they took me that first weekend. But they were also generous souls in their own way, and midst the teasing they gradually introduced me to the real joys of camping and fishing, so that after a few trips, the wilderness was no longer an alien but a welcome place to me.

It was scary at first, then fun. But it became a sustaining passion one weekend, in my second or third year at the camp, when we took a trip to a place called Foley Pond. To get there, you drive to the north end of Moosehead Lake, get off the paved road onto the dirt roads of the International Paper Company, and drive back about fifty miles or so into the forests that the company works for lumber. It's a wonderful area, with wildlife of every sort—birds, deer, porcupine, moose, and bear in abundance. Eventually, you come to a small stream, go up a rise, and, if you look carefully, you'll see the remains of what used to be a four-wheel drive road into Foley Pond, until it was sealed off by the paper company. This closing off of the road, whenever it happened long ago, was a wonderful thing. It meant that anyone who wants to fish Foley Pond must *really* want to fish Foley Pond, for it is now a five-mile hike, carrying a boat, into the pond. (One exception was that occasionally, some wealthy flatlanders had themselves flown into Foley by pontoon planes and dropped off there complete with canoes and camping gear—an event which, when we saw it, we greeted with undisguised contempt). My friends from Maine and I had eased the situation the previous summer by lugging in an old rowboat that someone didn't need any more and just leaving it there, tied up to a tree to which only we knew the way. But when you get to Foley, it's all worth it. The pond is perhaps a mile long and a half mile across. The trees come flush up to the water the whole way around the pond (which necessitates having a boat to fish it successfully) and the land rises up gradually but definitely on all sides to form mountains, the largest of which supports a fire tower at the top, the only sign of civilization visible from Foley. The pond, then, seems to sit at the bottom center of a huge bowl.

On the day I want to describe, my friends from Maine, Eben, Armand, Rufus, and I had been fishing most of the day, happily assuring ourselves by the good number of trout we were catching that we wouldn't have to resort to the peanut butter and jelly we brought along in case of bad luck. It had been a sunny, warm day, the blue sky articulated from time to time by billowy cumulus clouds. The water on Foley, when the wind is up, gets fairly rough, but when the wind dies down it can be as smooth as glass. It had varied during the day, and toward evening, approaching our limit of trout, we were beginning to talk of heading in. The wind, as it often does of an evening, completely died down, so that the water, utterly still now, became a crystal-clear mirror, reflecting in a subdued and lovely orange the surrounding mountains and the astonishing glow of the sun as it set over one of the mountains. Just then, a bluebird flew out, fluttered around our boat a few times, and hovered over us. I happened to look toward the shore at the end of the pond, and there, in the shimmering glow of the sunset, a large cow moose was feeding on the lily pads in the water, and beside her, her two young twins, probably born that spring.

Remember, I was in my middle twenties, at the peak of my romantic period. That experience, in its plenitude and peacefulness, struck me at the time as an epiphany, almost a counter-Heideggerian revelation of Being, Being not as withdrawal or absence, as the German would have it, but as fullness and totality, a whole in which I, this city kid, now felt utterly at home. It spoke to me of the meaning of immersion, and of oneness with nature, of sublime beauty and, at least for me at the time, a rare tranquility. Though I was there with my three Maine friends, the experience was also solitary, a harbinger of the seclusion I have found needful and appealing throughout my adulthood (I hardly would have spoken of such matters to my three older and more grizzly friends!). But the experience was not entirely a moment of youthful romanticism, for I have sought and found that same kind of experience again and again in fishing even to this day—in recent years usually along the Salmon River that bounds our land.

As a result no doubt of that moving experience, fishing for me is inseparable from the experience of natural beauty. I cannot imagine fishing along a city river, no matter how many fish I might catch. One of the attractions of fishing is that it does require concentration on the task at hand, tying on one's fly, casting successfully, noticing where the trout may be. But not a concentration that is all-encompassing; the experience is sufficiently slow and methodical, sufficiently demanding of patience, that one can notice and appreciate the beauty of the surroundings, and one can think, if only about being there. I almost always fish alone these days, seeking and finding that solitude that I've come to associate with tranquility and a kind of quiet contemplation. I especially love fishing the Salmon River along our land, a river I've come to know so well. I know the deep holes, the rapids, the flats. Though it changes from winter to winter, I quickly learn also where the fallen trees are, home often to trout and often as well to snagged hooks. That sense of familiarity in a place once strange has a deep appeal, as does, once more, the sense of recapitulating an activity and an involvement with the river once shared by Wangunk fishermen, and by earlier white settlers. Trout have a distinctive odor which stays on the hands when you handle them, and each Spring, with my first catch, the smell of trout on my hands recalls yet again all those sensations and thoughts and invites their familiar repetition (altogether more heady stuff, I suggest, than Proustian madeleines!).

Though it wasn't so early on, I've become one of those fishermen for whom actually catching lots of fish is a pleasant but unnecessary coda to the larger experience of fishing. I almost never think about "philosophy" in the technical sense while I'm fishing, but I've come to think of the experience as part of what it means to live philosophically. The experience, one might say, is thought-ful.

That is true in spades of farming, to which I came even later in life. Like most young couples, Anne and I spent our first six or so years of marriage living in city apartments, first in Toronto near the university, then in Hartford across the street from Trinity College. Our first house, where we lived for ten years, was in a heavily wooded area with not enough sunlight for a garden, though I don't remember ever thinking about that as a lack. Even when we moved to our present home, the house at first was set among dense red pines. But after a few years, the pines contacted a blight and began to die. Our little community had to make what at the time was the painful decision between simply letting them gradually die and fall—a potential danger to our houses—or having a lumberman cut them while the wood was still good. We chose the latter, and in a month or so our pain turned to delight as a beautiful view of the surrounding hills and the river below opened up from the field created by the cut trees. It also gave us six acres or so which we had to tend, and as part of that effort, the next summer Anne and I planted our first garden, a small patch perhaps twenty by twenty feet.

To begin a gardening career in one's forties may be something of a comment on social urbanization; it surely did not suggest that the activity would become, as it has, the source of such pleasure and sustenance. As soon as we began, I began to love every aspect of it. A family joke became that I even seemed to enjoy pulling weeds. Each year, I made the garden larger. Soon I needed to rent a rototiller to prepare the soil. A few years ago I bought my own. I now lust after a tractor. Wendell Berry became one of my favorite poets. The garden now approaches an acre's expanse; is an acre a large garden or a small farm? It is certainly larger than prudence would dictate, as it takes up large chunks of my time in the summer (time that I once jealously guarded for my writing), and yields far more than my family, relatives, and neighbors could possibly eat (the local food bank was the early beneficiary of this excess, until safety requirements demanded that they accept only packaged and canned goods). Until very recently, I gave hardly a single thought to retirement from professional philosophy and

teaching. Now, occasionally, I do, but when I do so my thoughts are almost entirely focused on the additional time that will be freed up for farming and fishing.

There's something about working the soil that I find at once irresistible and deeply satisfying. As previous essays have indicated, I've been an active athlete all my life and I still find some way to work out almost every day. But the sense of tiredness one gets from an afternoon working in the garden is like no other tiredness. Is it that the fatigue is accompanied by a sense of worthwhile labor? Possibly, though I certainly never felt that the time spent in various sports was not worthwhile. Perhaps it's the sheer childlike fun of getting dirty. Or the sense of purposefulness gleaned from the anticipation that one's labor will yield tangible, edible results. Or is it the romantic sense of oneness with the coursing of the seasons and the immersion in the tenuous requisites of farming, rain at the right time, sun, and manure for the soil? I know this: my livelihood is in no sense dependent on my crop yield—in fact, I'm sure I lose money every summer—but my feeling of anxiety during summer droughts or late spring frosts is palpable. It's the closest a man of the city can come, perhaps, to the simple but moving fate once that of us all, to be dependent on the weather and the elements, to truly need them for our life projects. The difference between my experience of rain during the school year and in the summer is striking, and perhaps revealing. During the school year, a day of rain is almost always a nuisance. Clothes and shoes will get wet, catching colds more likely, avoiding the outdoors a near necessity. But in the summer, especially if it hasn't rained for a few days, the project of farming changes everything. Rain becomes something hoped for, and, when it comes, welcomed with delight. I've learned to smell the coming rain on the air, and to rejoice in it.

And in the soil. I don't quite understand the simple pleasure one takes in feeling soil in one's hands, but that lack of understanding doesn't interfere with the enjoyment itself. I love just to *hold* soil, to turn it over in my hands, let it run through my fingers, even get it on my face when I wipe the sweat off my forehead with soil-laden hands. How could something so simple and so

out of keeping with urban manners be so pleasant? The same is true with the summer heat, usually, for me as for most people, a nuisance or burden in the middle of summer. But while in my garden it almost never bothers me. I learned early on the farmer's and cowboy's wisdom, to wear a long sleeve shirt, long pants, and a hat, no matter how hot it got. Sure, you sweat like crazy and your clothes get drenched, but the heat simply doesn't bother you as much. And somehow, it seems to add to that delicious feeling of being part of the process, of involving yourself intimately with the land, perhaps as we were meant to be.

There's a special pleasure in sowing the seed, in the cautious calculations of where to sow what, taking account of sun, shade, soil makeup, and the location of crops the previous year. Part of that pleasure, surely, is in the anticipation, of thinking about how, in a month or two, this barren soil will be fruitful. If all goes well. But I even enjoy broadcasting the hairy vetch and clover I plant each autumn to renew the soil for the coming Spring. That too is a pleasure of anticipation, though a distant one.

But the family joke about the joys of weeding aside, I think I find most enjoyable the tilling of the soil, wonderful metaphor for thinking. Like fishing, tilling does give one time to think, and the activity of tilling itself, turning over and thereby deepening and enriching the soil, invites a similar turning over, deepening and enriching of the events of one's life. Like fishing, too, I think of it largely as an internal experience of solitude, though often enough Anne is working at my side. Our conversations while farming, I find, are more reticent than usual, often one sentence exchanges about the soil, or the weather, or where to plant what. Working the soil invites one's thoughts to turn inward, and outward only to the task at hand. Is it thinking that I do while I work the soil, or something more like meditation?

Curiously perhaps, the actual harvesting of the fruits of the land is one of the lesser joys I find in farming. Of course I love to eat the fresh vegetables, succulent beyond anything one could buy even at a roadside stand. Anne and I become de facto vegetarians in the summer, simply because the food is so good.

But for some reason, I don't take the same sort of satisfaction in harvesting the crops as in the other work of farming. Is this a farmer's version of the artist's common experience of the completed work as "over and done with," teaching us that the true meaning is in the activity, the process? As often as not, Anne does the harvesting for the evening meal.

Each winter, usually early in February, Anne and I gather the seed catalogues and spend several evenings paging through them, making the decisions, which we treat with completely unwarranted importance, as to what seeds we'll order for the coming spring. In the stark and cold winter nights, there's a surprising delight in this palpable anticipation that spring will come, that we'll once again participate in the natural cycle of growing things, no longer a necessity of life, to be sure, but perhaps even more of a pleasure for that.

Addendum

Regarding fishing, as I reach the autumn of my years, I'm still an avid fisherman, but a number of things have changed. I used to follow the Indigenous American adage, "Never kill anything you're not going to eat," and so I would limit my catch to what I and my family planned to eat that night. Over the years, though, I became persuaded to the "catch and release" philosophy, and now follow it exclusively. Partly this arises out of a decision that it's best to let the fish keep on living in the name of conservation. But also, I recall well a conversation I had a few years ago with a guide I was with in northern New Hampshire, fishing the sources of what becomes the Connecticut River. We were in an area rich in deer, bear, and moose, and I asked him (a local) if he also hunted as well as fished. He replied no, and I asked him why. "Because I haven't figured out a way to shoot and release them," he replied. Around the same time, I began turning exclusively to fly fishing with unbarbed hooks—partly because it was more challenging and active, but mostly because, since the fly virtually always hooks the fish on its gristly lip and the fish almost never swallows the fly, much less damage is done to the fish, which can immediately be put back into the water to continue its life.

Second, as time went on and I began to lose agility, it became increasingly difficult—and frankly, dangerous—to wade alone while fishing, as I had long preferred. I gradually had to limit myself to calm and not very deep waters. So I made the decision to make my fishing less solitary, safer, and much more expensive: I began fishing with guides. This meant giving up the solitary dimension of the experience that had long appealed to me. But I gained the most enjoyable experience of conversation and education with the various guides with whom I fished. These guides tend to be a most intriguing group, full of knowledge, yes, but also full of stories and good humor.

When we moved to Massachusetts, I began as well to change my fishing locations from the Salmon and Farmington rivers in Connecticut to two rivers in western Massachusetts, the Deerfield and the Swift rivers, the Swift in central, the Deerfield in western Massachusetts, two relatively accessible rivers from Boston. Both of them, like the Farmington in Connecticut, are tailwater rivers, meaning that the water flows from dams upstream. Since the water is released from the bottom of the dams, it means that the water stays relatively cold all summer. And since trout, for which I fish now almost exclusively, are sensitive creatures who cannot flourish in water much above 65 degrees, this means that trout can really flourish in these rivers. More importantly, I was lucky enough to find two guides, the Harrison brothers, Tom and Dan, who grew up fishing those two rivers, seem to know where every trout in the river lives, and who now have a guide business that does float trips in specialized boats that float down the rivers. This pretty much takes care of both the danger element in wading as well as the limitations on where in the river I could fish. Indeed, the boats could take us to parts of the river pretty much inaccessible to waders. This means that in addition to the greater safety over wading, the float trips enhance the aesthetics of the fishing experience. Especially when we fish the upper reaches of the Deerfield near the dam, we're way out of phone reception, we see all sorts of wildlife, and the landscape takes on the look of the wilderness of northern Maine that I so loved in my youthful initiation to fishing.

A final enhancement to my "senior" fishing experience: it's not just that I'm usually fishing with one of the Harrisons in their boat now; I'm almost always accompanied by another member of the family—usually my older son, Chris, now an accomplished fly fisherman, but occasionally my other son, Craig, and one or both of my two youngest grandsons, Zeke and Elias, the latter of whom, now 11 years old, opened his fishing career a year ago by catching 17 trout! (He counted them, I don't!).

Regarding farming, with our move to the Boston area my farmable land has been reduced from over an acre to three small plots on three sides of our house, each of them perhaps 6 feet by 20 or so. When we first moved here, I promptly planted tomato plants and other vegetables in the sunniest of the three plots, but Anne, wise woman, decided to send dirt samples to the state Agriculture department, who before long informed us that the soil around our 100+ year old house was full of lead! Out came the tomato plants, and we now plant exclusively flower plants in the ground. Our son Chris, however, built two small, raised gardens for us, which now sit in our driveway (the sunniest part of our yard) and supply us with at least a few tomatoes and other vegetables each year. Of course this is not the same as our large gardens of yore. Something more like a nostalgia trip for both of us, but an enjoyable one nevertheless.

CHAPTER 5

Parenthood

"It makes no small difference, then, whether we form habits of one kind or another from our very youth; it makes a great difference, or rather all the difference."

ARISTOTLE

IN THE BEST CIRCUMSTANCES, the now cliched African proverb, "it takes a whole village to raise a child," is no doubt true, and one only wishes that it were conscientiously pursued more often in the modern world. Probably the closest most of us come to this ideal is that in occasional families, the whole extended family raises the child. But even that is seldom possible anymore. The best most of us can hope for these days, and even this not often enough, is that the whole nuclear family, and not just one parent, raises the child. That was my situation as a child and as a parent, and so will be the primary model I discuss.

Almost everyone's first experience of parenthood, of course, is as a child. My own parents raised me, at least as I saw it, with distinctly different attitudes, attitudes which formed the grid in terms of which I made my own choices much later as a parent. From a remarkably early age, I remember having the sense that my father raised me with the overarching goal of freeing me, of raising me to be independent, free to become who I wanted to be. Long before my mother was willing, my father regularly allowed me to take some new step into freedom, whether it was riding my bike out of the neighborhood, driving throughout the sometimes dangerous streets of Philadelphia in search of sandlot basketball games, staying out later at night, going to the Atlantic seashore alone in high school, or choosing to be a philosophy major in college, against my parents expectations and probably their hopes. Always, I had the sense that my father wanted to give me as much freedom as I could possibly handle, even with the risks that that freedom occasionally incurred. Not that he wasn't a very strict father; on issues of behavior, manners, character traits, my father was as demanding as could be, and now if not then I thank him for it. But on the matter of allowing me to break free of parental constraints, he was, in the literal sense, a liberal (Father, do not turn over in your grave at this epithet! I use it in a strict sense that I hope you find acceptable!).

My mother, on the other hand, seemed guided primarily by the desire to protect me, or perhaps more selfishly, to keep me as her own. I prefer the former interpretation, since, at least consciously, her intentions were entirely noble. She too, as much as my father, wanted what was best for me, and she thought that what was best for me was to keep me safe from harm's way. And the danger, as she saw it, was everywhere out of her sight.

These polar but equally well-intentioned attitudes caused tensions, probably more than I knew. My own experience of those tensions was unfortunate, for it played out, as I grew through high school, as a conspiracy between my father and me to keep my mother uninformed of my real activities. In the summer between my sophomore and junior years in high school (that is, as a sixteen year old), I started making the two-hour drive from Philadelphia to the New Jersey seashore for the weekend, something my mother would have found completely unacceptable. With my father's condoning, I would tell Mother I was staying at a friend's house, tell my father where I'd be at the shore, and leave for the weekend. This became an unfortunate pattern of my way of dealing with my parents: "Tell Dad what I'm doing, tell Mom what she needs to know." Over time, this generated in me an all-too easy tolerance for certain kinds of deception, obviously a totally unacceptable solution to a genuine and honest problem: I had two parents, both with the best of intentions and equally desirable goals—to free me and to protect me—which, at least as they played out in my family, often seemed incompatible.

There may be certain gender associations at work in these traits. The stereotypes of the over-protective mother and the more independence-granting father are well-known. But they are hardly universal. One need only think of the hysterical and tyrannical athletic father, dominating his son's or daughter's athletic development—forcing him or her into this sport, this position, this school, this team—to recognize that not every father is moved primarily by the desire to free his children to become who they want to be. Nor, equally obviously, is every mother over-protective or even as protective as a parent should be.

Gender inscription aside, it was only much later, as an adult and parent myself, that I come to appreciate the legitimacy of both my parents' concerns and the dilemma that legitimacy presented me. For what was perhaps too polarized in the two of them was gathered as an internal conflict in me, and I came in good measure to think of those two commitments, freedom and protection, as the guiding poles between which I would make my own parental decisions. But of that more later.

Mine was perhaps the last generation for whom having children was taken as more or less the "natural" consequence of getting married, and not the subject of an elaborate and sometimes wrenching weighing of pros and cons. I was first struck by this when I noticed, years ago, my own students, hardly a decade older than me, as they went into their careers and got married, going through what were often troubled and in any case immensely complicated decision processes about whether or not to have children. Nor was this simply a matter of more women starting careers and experiencing their own conflict between career and family aspiration. As often as not, it was the male partner, troubled by a reluctance to pay the price in time from his career goals that he suspected, rightly, child raising would entail. In any case, such ruminations were not part of Anne and my lives, nor of most of our friends. At most, the issue was how soon after marriage could one afford the cost of childbirth and rearing; as soon as things seemed financially clear, one went ahead with it. Some of us didn't wait that long.

The upshot, for those of my generation, was that becoming a parent was rarely a result of careful, thoughtful, or profound reflection. It was, again, taken as "natural." Consequently, our movement into parenthood and the principles that informed our parental decisions (including the one to become parents at all) were not the result, very often at least, of prior, explicitly reflective judgments. Aside from the above-mentioned sentiments concerning freedom and protection, I can recall not a single self-consciously articulated "principle" of child-rearing with which I went into parenthood. We tended to raise our children "on the fly," as it were. Was that a fault corrected by a more careful, calculating next generation? Or a virtue? Is this a matter that, in good Socratic fashion, is so important that it should be entered into only after the most careful reflection and weighing of the pros and cons? Or, in more Aristotelian fashion, is it better as a character trait so deeply imbued in one by the time of adulthood that a self-conscious decision is hardly needed, as was the case with Anne and me? Certainly, both the decision to become parents and the weighing of principled decisions about child raising were less Angst-full for Anne and me than for many of my students.

Not that my experience of being a father was a series of mindless responses. But I did tend to face up to issues *in situ*. And I found, again and again, that my reactions and decisions were informed by my own responses to my experience of childhood with my parents. My father tended to hold his emotions in; it was sometimes hard to know if he was angry at me or just preoccupied. Not so with my mother, who wore her emotions most visibly on her face and in her voice. I decided my mother's way was better, and made an effort to always let our two boys know explicitly how I felt about this or that action. On the other hand, my mother, when she became angry at my brother and me for some no doubt egregious misdemeanor, would sometimes refuse to speak to us for days; I remember being repelled by that behavior, and determined never to hold a grudge toward my own boys when they transgressed, to let the emotions out and be done with it. And throughout their childhood, I found my decisions about what they could or could not do wending their way between the legitimate requirements of independence and protection characteristic of my respective parents.

This I believe. There is a depth and intensity of emotion, of life experience, available in being a parent that is true of no other of life's projects, neither career nor other encounters. Let me modify that; it is not just a quantitative matter of depth or intensity; it is also a certain quality of experience that I am tempted to call unique to parenthood. Perhaps it has something to do with the complex of ingredients; responsibility, love, hope, aspiration, concern, fear, frustration, disappointment, exhilaration. Politically incorrect though it may be to say it, I do not believe that depth and quality is available to those who choose not to have children. One small example; if one takes parenthood with any seriousness whatsoever, it is simply impossible to preserve the kind of self-centeredness often characteristic of our pre-parenthood days and often exhibited, so far as I can see, by those without the "burden" of children.

To be sure, not all that depth and intensity is positive or enjoyable. In Anne and my case, our first son, Christopher, proved at a very early age to be peculiarly accident prone, so much so that it became something of a macabre family joke. By the time he was thirteen years old, he had had thirteen trips to the hospital emergency room in whatever town we lived—an average of one a year! Some of those trips were horrendous. I recall one early one, though not the first, when he was just a year old, and, as I was presenting Anne with Valentine's Day roses, he crawled into the closet under the sink and swallowed some bleach. Needless to say, this caused intense screaming, and as Anne and I rushed him to the hospital in Toronto where I was teaching at the time, he gradually cried himself to sleep. Anne and I, however, had no idea that it was simply sleep into which he was falling, and feared altogether worse events. The abject terror of the feared death of one's child, let me say, is a feeling I would wish on no one. Even in retrospect, long after the event, it remains powerful and sobering.

Later, as Chris grew up and the number of trips increased, not only Anne and I but Christopher himself became almost cavalier about it. Once, when he was perhaps seven or eight, the two of us were playing basketball together, and, as I happened to lean over him, he suddenly jumped up into my face. My front tooth broke off into his head, resulting in a trip to the emergency room for both of us. But by that time, and no doubt in part because we didn't perceive the situation as especially threatening, the visit was much less hysterical. If fact, while waiting in the emergency room I was startled to see Chris go over and comfort several other children waiting to have their own injuries treated!

With the birth of our second son, Craig, we began to learn the crucial wisdom that one cannot apply the lessons of raising one child to another. I often wonder at the occasional parents who insist proudly that they "always treat their children the same." I don't see how such a thing would be possible, much less desirable, so different are they and at such a young age do those differences appear. It began to strike Anne and me by the time he was just a few weeks old that Craig was a very different person than his brother. Though no less active and athletic, he avoided the tendency to accidents so typical of Christopher. But the real differences were in personality. Chris, very much in the tradition of his paternal grandfather, tended to keep his emotions under control. It was often difficult to tell what he was really thinking, and almost impossible to discipline him, since one could rarely tell whether the attempted discipline had had the desired effect. But Craig, in next to no time, was demonstrating an overt expression of his emotions that was as honest as it was explosive. Two such distinct people could not possibly be fairly treated the same, and we soon learned not to try, though we often lamented that so few of the hard-won lessons gleaned from raising Christopher could be applied directly to raising Craig.

One of the many blessings of being a college teacher is that one's working hours are not so rigorously stipulated as is the case with many occupations. Given that so much of a professor's time is spent preparing lectures and writing books and articles, one has the option of going to the office every day and doing all that work in one's college office or electing instead to do much of one's class preparation and independent writing at home. Early on, I determined that it would be far easier to convince my family to allow me certain periods of uninterrupted work than to convince a much larger battery of colleagues, administrators, and students. So I fell into a pattern of doing a good amount of my preparation at home, which meant, in turn, that I was able to be at home more than most fathers, which meant, finally, that I was able to participate much more actively and regularly in the raising of our children than is vouchsafed to most fathers. And that was indeed a blessing. To be sure, it required a sometimes delicate balancing act between actively participating in the child-raising and preserving sufficient time for myself to do my work. But that, after all, was part of raising the boys, to teach them that while they were in many ways the center of Anne and my lives, we did both have independent interests which required time, and those interests had to be honored by the children. As they grew to be preschoolers and elementary students able to play in the neighborhood, we developed a guideline for the conditions under which Daddy could be interrupted from his work for a crisis: no blood, no interruptions! Our sons, now adults, tease me about that rule to this day. It resulted in my hearing some hilarious childhood conversations outside the window of my study from time to time. The boys' neighborhood friends, whose fathers by and large went to work early in the morning and returned late in the evening, didn't understand our situation well at all. They would often suggest that Chris or Craig come into the house to get me for some project or other. Our boys would reply that I was working, whereupon the reply would come that I certainly wasn't working because they had seen me in the house! But the fact that Anne and I both had occupations—Anne with her pottery and me with my philosophy—that allowed us to do significant amounts of our work at home meant that a necessary part of the boys' up-bringing was teaching them to honor our independent interests and the requirements of those interests. I like to believe that their relative lack of self-centeredness as adults is in part a function of that democratic lesson learned so early on.

I think of this often when discussions of contemporary feminism arise. I rarely hear this mentioned anymore, but I remember well that one of the primary feminist recommendations of the 1960s was that, instead of the typical family situation where the mother stayed home all week to take care of the kids and the father went to work all week, both jobs would be split more or less evenly. We would have to reorganize America's corporate work structure so that the typical business week of an individual would be about 25 hours instead of 40, but each parent would work that 25 hours, staying home to mind the family for the other time. Since Anne and I were living out something of a prototype of that recommendation, we were utterly enthusiastic about it, and dismayed to see, as time went by, the other, altogether more stressful alternative become the norm: both the mother and the father working 40+ hour weeks while the kids were placed in day-care centers. There were no doubt good reasons for that decision, not the least being the economic necessity of two full salaries as family economic situations became more tenuous. But I suspect that was not the whole of the story. Part of the reason also seemed to be a certain greed, for bigger houses, more expensive cars, more luxurious vacations, and a corresponding obliviousness to what they were missing and Anne and I were being blessed with, the experience of raising our children, in a full sense, together.

This national decision in favor of two full salaries must be coupled, I think, with the parallel phenomenon of suburbaniza-tion and the long commute to work. In an earlier epoch, even though the father was the almost exclusive "breadwinner" and the mother responsible for the running of the home, it remained the case in the typical family that the father was, after all, close by; on the farm, in the shop next door or downstairs, in the factory down the street. That meant that the father was home until a few minutes before work, home for lunch, home soon after work, and in any case available in case a crisis should arise. Nowadays, that is rarely true of either parent, whose jobs take them an hour or more commute from the day care center that is effectively raising their children. What strikes me about this is only in part the connections that might be made between these phenomena and the much-lamented loss of family values, breakdown of the family, etc. My own very different experience as a father leads me to lament the loss in richness to parents, and especially to fathers, who are not afforded the opportunity to experience in its full depth the meaning of parenthood.

This loss took a very concrete form in our town, which I learned only from our boys as they grew up and began informing us from time to time of some of the differences between our family and those of their friends. Following a tradition of both Anne and my parents, one which we took not at all as a peculiar tradition but a natural phenomenon, we made the dinner hour a primary time of the day for family comraderies. Even though I typically saw the children and Anne more during the day than most fathers, dinner time was still that special hour when we all gathered together not to resolve this or that crisis or to pursue a career project, but to share with each other the events of the day and, as time went on and the boys took on views of their own, our reactions to those events. We went to often extraordinary lengths to preserve that time together. As the boys grew up and their athletic ability became evident, they began to play on organized teams, first little league, then the interscholastic teams of their public school. Their practices, and especially their games, often interfered with our normal dinner hour. In response, we simply adjusted our dinner hour to whatever time of the day was available for us all. It might be as early as 5:30 or as late as 10:00 pm, after the games were over. But it never occurred to us *not* to have dinner together. Again, we took all this not as anything unusual but as the normal thing to do. Only in time did the boys report to us in one conversation or another that we were virtually the only family among their friends who had a common dinner hour. The norm among their friends seemed to be that late in the afternoon the mother would heat something up on the stove, and whenever anyone was hungry they could go into the kitchen and get something to eat. This stunned Anne and me, for whom the sharing of the events of the day was such an important part of the dinner hour. It struck me as a very powerful symbol, and perhaps not just a symbol but a symptom, of the reality of the breakdown of the American family that one reads so much about these days. Once again, part of the reason for the "breakdown of the family dinner" in our town was no doubt economic. In a for the most part working-class town, both parents usually had jobs if not by choice by necessity, and when that is so, the preparation and organizing of a family dinner becomes more complicated. But if so, I lament its loss none the less for its necessity.

Was I a "strict" parent? I think I followed, with some modifications, the parental path of my father. I was and would be again quite demanding on matters of conduct and manners. The boys still occasionally remind me, because it was so different from the families of their peers, that I would not tolerate their "talking back" to Anne or me, nor the use of profanity as responses to our demands. Anne and I did our best to inculcate virtues in the boys to the extent (and it is only an extent) that we could. In doing so, we learned the truth of Aristotle's conviction that the development of virtues is largely a matter of developing certain character traits, habits of conduct, which will stay with one long after the watchfulness of parents has ended. I had the clear sense, sometimes with relief, sometimes with frustration, that the extent to which we could "raise the kids with the right values" was largely over by the time they were in their mid-teens. After that, it was pretty much a matter of letting them go to become who they are.

A particularly delicate issue in childrearing, for me if not for Anne, centered on the matter of athletic involvement. As previous essays have made clear enough, I was a passionately committed athlete for whom athletics was the center of my youth and early manhood. It went without saying that I would encourage the boys enthusiastically to enjoy athletics. But, given my background, I was probably a classic instance of the danger of a parent trying to "relive his youth" through his children's athletic involvement. Fortunately, I was aware of the problem and, thanks to witnessing some of the horror stories one so often hears about youth sports involving overzealous parents, I was keenly committed to not being that kind of parent. So I did my best to give enthusiastic encouragement while avoiding even the hint of coercion. Chris and Craig can say best whether I succeeded. But I have to say that I took no small pleasure in the fact that as they both grew up, though they both became very adept—in fact high school all-stars—in basketball, my own sport of concentration, the sport in which they became truly outstanding—all-state athletes and eventually college players—was soccer, a sport I had never played. At least I had not "forced" them into basketball!

At the beginning of this essay I lamented the decline of those situations in which the African proverb might be true, that "the whole village" does raise the child. Yet in a certain sense, for better or worse, there remains a kernel of truth in it. As soon as the boys were old enough to begin playing with the neighborhood children—and that is when they were barely three—the influence of "the village" began to kick in. Some of our neighbors had rather different standards and styles of life than we did, and the boys, as are all children, were therefore subjected to very different ideas and influences from Anne and mine. As always, some of those differences were desirable and fruitful, others not. We had some explaining to do when a neighboring father, in an effort to dissuade the local children from climbing or reaching down into the street sewers, told them that "the devil" lived down there. More complex was our effort to convince the boys, against the clear sentiment of most of the parents on the street, that fighting was not an appropriate way to settle differences.

East Hampton, Connecticut, the town in which we live and raised our boys, has the basic culture of the rural working class. A less sympathetic observer might call it "redneck." To be sure, the last decade has occasioned the encroachment of a group of more affluent commuters to Hartford, some twenty-five miles away. But they have not yet changed the town's basic cultural character, which, not to put too fine a point on it, is very "rough and ready." That character has many wonderful charms for which we remain grateful: an almost total lack of snobbery, very little "keeping up with the Joneses," thus an appealing unpretentiousness, and the expectation that what financial gain you might obtain is and should be the result of hard work. These qualities, I'm happy to say, have apparently deeply and irrevocably influenced our boys, even as they have moved into more affluent local cultures. There was also a dark side to the town's culture, however, which we soon learned we had to resist. Like many if not most working-class towns, racism was all too rampant; we had to encourage the boys from early on not to give in to that. Also characteristic of too much of the town's culture was an acceptance of violence as an appropriate and natural response to disagreement or anger, as well as to strangers.

We could either leave town or respond to these negative features. Though Anne and I did at times consider moving, we settled instead on a different strategy. After all, our own daily cultures were significantly different from that of the town in which we lived. I worked in the academic community of Trinity College, Anne, as an artist, worked with a coterie of other artists, including, happily, a few local ones. At our family dinner gatherings and at other times, we made a point of making the differences in cultural stances explicit and the theme of our discussions. We encouraged the boys to tell us what had happened that day, and we would discuss not only the events themselves but their ethical implications. In doing so, I think we enabled the boys to see that they had ethical choices which should be the result of reflection, that they were at least in part, and more so as they grew older, responsible for choosing what standards, convictions, and codes of behavior they would allow to influence them.

I recall conversations of this sort as early as their participation in little league, when occasionally their mates would overtly cheat or intimidate other players. Worse, they had a few experiences of those now notorious "little league fathers," who preached the conviction, absurd in general but all the more for children, that "winning is everything." But the most sustained conversations, and in the long run the most powerful, came as they reached high school and began to play on the interscholastic teams. There, with the greater intensity and sense of a stake that the various inter-town rivalries engendered, they were confronted with coaches, team-mates, and parents whose ideas of the meaning of competition and the responsibilities of athletic sportsmanship were very different from our own. We gradually developed an unspoken family custom of having a family gathering at home after most of the high school games (often over a very late meal), where we would rehash the events of the game, and decide what lessons, athletic and ethical, we wanted to draw from them.

If there is a general lesson to be drawn from those family gatherings, I think it is the value of explicitly discussing ethical issues with our children, not abstractly in polite aphorisms, but concretely in terms of the real situations they had just encountered. In those discussions, the boys learned that how they conducted themselves, the principles by which they led their lives, had to be self-conscious choices for which they became responsible, even if, as Aristotle knew so well, they began to be influenced by them long before they could choose. To the extent that we can show our children that they must *decide* how they will act, that they had best do so by reflecting on the alternatives, and that they are finally responsible for their actions, we better prepare them to become free, and good.

And now I'm a grandfather! Just as I took this and rejected that from my own parents, I now watch with interest and delight as Christopher picks and chooses from Anne and me how he will conduct his own fatherhood. No doubt Craig will do the same in due time. Perhaps because of all those trips to the emergency room, Chris seems more cautious and protective of his two sons than I was of him. At least so far (his oldest son is not quite six years old as I write) he seems less given to strict discipline than I was. But I note with delight that he goes out of his way to be sure to spend as much time as possible with his children, anxious, insistent perhaps, to have the same intense experience of fatherhood that I had with him. And he's inviting them into the joys of athletics with the same enthusiasm and absence of coercion that I sought in raising him. Needless to say, to the extent that I can be, I'm a co-conspirator.

Addendum

We now have seven grandchildren, ranging in age, as I write this, from the early thirties to the early teens. Not surprisingly, they have all been, and all remain, strongly athletic. They have been and still are the source of great enjoyment for Anne and me, watching them play in their various games on weekends. Soccer seems to have become the family go-to sport, though Alexandra, Chris' youngest, became an All-American gymnast at the University of Kentucky, and Phoebe, Craig's oldest, made "ultimate frisbee" her sport of choice in college, after experiencing both soccer and crew in high school. As I think about their athletic experience, however, I'm deeply struck, and frankly troubled, by a cultural phenomenon in the United States that has deeply changed their experience of sport from that of my boys and especially my own. This has to do, I think, very much with the *limits* of parenting. For, although the younger boys did (and will) play soccer for their high school teams, the real locus of their athletic activity has become, sometimes almost exclusively, the various athletic "clubs" to which they belong (in the case of basketball, the various teams are not called "clubs," although they function independently of any educational system, just as the soccer clubs do). Now these clubs are no doubt for the most part well-intentioned: to give youngsters—especially the athletically gifted ones—opportunities to play and improve. The players are mostly "coached," especially at the younger levels, by parents. This phenomenon is so widespread that, at least in soccer and basketball, the two sports about which I am moderately knowledgeable, college coaches now concentrate their recruiting efforts less on the high school teams and predominantly on the club teams.

This phenomenon has two features that deeply trouble me. The first is obvious: well-meaning as the parents who organize and coach the clubs may be, their level of expertise not surprisingly varies all over the place. Not to mention their level of fairness when, as is often the case, their own children are participants on the team. But a second feature troubles me much more. This phenomenon has brought about a situation in which the children's athletic lives are in many cases virtually *entirely* organized by adults. Not only do the parents drive their children to the fields and courts where the games are played—often a good distance from their homes—but the parents are also the administers and coaches of the teams as well. The result, and this marks a huge difference from the youthful experience of my own children and even more so of my own, is that in many cases almost the entire athletic lives of these children today are organized, coached, refereed, and overseen by adults. The days of the pick-up basketball, soccer, or baseball game, where a group of kids show up at a playground on their own, choose sides evenly to make it a good game, referee their own games, resolve their own disputes, in short, play under their own auspices, are, with one exception that I shall presently mention, largely gone.

I regard this as a significant cultural loss. In the case of my boys who grew into their athletic prowess in the 70's and 80's, there was a Little League in our town, but that was it. Basketball, soccer, football, indeed all the rest of their athletic choices were almost entirely up to them. And the Little league was in some measure the subject of sardonic comment, for the annual "All-Star" team chosen to play the corresponding teams from other towns, was inevitably composed for the most part of the sons of the various team coaches. In the case of my own youth, the situation was even more fluid. If there was a Little League in Lansdowne, Pennsylvania, I didn't even know about it. We played sports almost every day, but those games were *always* a matter of our own doing. Where we would meet to play, what the teams would be, how the infractions would be called, all of this was up to us. Here is just one example of such an ethically laden decision: when one is playing playground basketball without referees, the problem of who calls the inevitable fouls soon arises. Either the person who gets fouled calls the foul, or the person who commits the foul does so. In Philadelphia when I was growing up, the person committing the foul makes the call, and "gives" the foul to the player fouled. There is an obvious danger involved with this decision: if, in my judgment, I get fouled on a given play and the person fouling me does not "give" the foul, that is, call the foul on himself, then on the next play I may be tempted to foul *him* and not call the foul. If this continues (and no doubt, it sometimes did), it could result in a pretty rough and tumble game. Nevertheless, we held firmly to this somewhat macho principle, that no "man" would call a foul in his own behalf. I was therefore surprised and somewhat appalled when I moved to New England and discovered that the rule in this area was to call a foul for oneself if you believed you were fouled on a given play. The obvious danger here was the converse of the "Philadelphia" principle: if I'm guarding someone and they call a foul on me when I didn't think I fouled him, I might be tempted to do the same, and the game would devolve—as it no doubt sometimes did—into an endless series of foul-calling, what we on the misogynistic playgrounds of Philadelphia called "girl-scout" basketball. Think of all the ethical issues implicit in this otherwise hardly world-shaking decision about how to self-referee basketball games.

All this I believe was the source of invaluable lessons of life: of getting along with each other, of resolving disputes, of distributing "goods" (that is, the best players) equitably, all this and more we learned from organizing our own athletic lives. Today, the only place I still see this take place is occasionally when I drive past urban outdoor basketball courts, mostly in minority neighborhoods, where it seems that such self-guided athletic moments still happen (A remarkable book has been written about this largely urban and minority phenomenon: I heartily recommend reading Onaje X. O. Woodbine's *Black Gods of the Ashalt: Religion, Hip-Hop, and Street Basketball)*. I drive past these courts with delight and no little nostalgia.

I lament deeply this cultural loss. I don't hesitate to say that this self-organizing of our sporting lives was part of our *education.* We learned on these myriad occasions invaluable lessons in independence, in ethics, in the resolution of disputes, in short, lessons in living. I still believe we should allow our children these educational opportunities, and I also believe that these lessons cannot and should not be *imposed* on our children by parents, even if well-meaning ones.

CHAPTER 6

Friendship

"Compassion for the friend should conceal itself under a hard shell, and you should break a tooth on it. That way it will have delicacy and sweetness."

NIETZSCHE

ABOUT FRIENDSHIP MUCH AND perhaps enough has been written. This is one of the few topics in this collection on which well-known philosophers have written extensively. Beginning at least with Plato's *Lysis* and Aristotle's *Nicomachean Ethics*, philosophers have recognized in friendship an important issue for philosophic reflection. I do not intend to develop here a rival or augmenting "theory" of friendship. Rather, in the spirit of the previous essays and in partial imitation of the drama of Plato's *Lysis*, I shall relate a number of experiences of friendship which I believe exhibit, or show forth, the power of friendship and of certain understandings of it.

My first friend, surely, was my brother. Our friendship at least in our youth, was largely based on play, in the sense that the encounters that were the locus of that friendship were predominantly those of playing together. And before long, as previous essays have made manifest, that play was primarily in the mode of competitive athletics. Often enough, especially as we grew up into organized interscholastic sports, we were teammates, and our friendship had about it the explicitly cooperative flavor of teammates in a common pursuit of success. But in truth, as often as not my brother and I found ourselves alone together on playgrounds, at odd hours, when no one else was there, and our friendship was manifested in a directly competitive mode; we played hour after hour, day after day, in "one-on-one" games with each other, mostly basketball, but sometimes, when no court was available, other sports and games as well. Even as young adults, when I was in graduate school and Art still in college, whenever we both came home for family gatherings, my brother and I would head to a court for a few games of one-on-one. It was the way we reaffirmed our kinship, and we both loved it. Playing together, playing with each other, playing against each other: those experiences were inseparable from my first deep experience of friendship, and they have deeply influenced my sense of friendship and my expectations about it ever since.

Which is to say, early on I came to experience friendship in the spirit of Nietzsche's remark above, as what I will call a "demand relationship." That is, I came to understand friendship as a relationship in which one always *expected the best* from each other. This was true when we were playing on the same team, where in order for us to win we each had to play our best and came to trust each other to make that maximum effort each game. But it was no less true when we played *against* each other, where we soon learned that in order to have the most fun we both had to go all out to win. If one of us "screwed around," the other would often get angry, and with good reason: the offending laggard was not living up to the demands of genuine competitive friendship. This, I later came to believe, is the profound significance of the word "competition:" com-petitio: "to inquire or strive together." Competitive friendships are indeed profoundly cooperative. Each demands of oneself and of the other that they be the best that they can. More than that, I *need* the other to do the best that he can in order for me to attain to my best. So I demand both of myself and my friend that we be the best we can.

This is the sense I developed early on of friendship as a demand relationship. And before long, that sense extended from our play lives to the rest of our lives as well, and eventually, as I said, to my very expectation of what genuine friendship is.

This, of course, is not what many, perhaps most, think friendship is. To the contrary, friendship is often regarded as quite the opposite, as a *non*-demanding relationship in which we do *not* "impose" our expectations, "values," or opinions on our friend. After all, does not competition of any sort inevitably lead not to friendship but to alienation? Other people (parents, teachers, bosses) may "hassle" us, but friends "let each other do their own thing." I know well of that understanding of friendship, but it is simply not true to my experience. It strikes me, in the end, as a rather superficial experience of friendship.

From my brother, and founded on that experience, my early experiences of friendship with others were usually with teammates, and took the same reciprocally competitive, and therefore demanding, form. One early memory of how that demand relationship with a teammate showed itself outside of the confines of sports participation now seems quite comical, though at the time it seemed momentous to us both. It was in my junior year in high school. Most of my teammates that year were seniors, though one other player, the center on the team and my good friend, was also a junior. There was a distinct difference in values and lifestyle between the group of seniors and we two juniors on that team. The seniors all drank to excess, (even, on one memorable occasion, on the day of a game!), were utterly marginal students, and generally regarded as "troublemakers" in the school. One evening, they had all got drunk, gone down to Race Street in Philadelphia, and got tattoos on their arms—an act that was greeted with considerably more shock in those days than it would be now. This caused much consternation and embarrassment to school officials, who made the offending players wear tape over their tattoos during the games. Nevertheless, one night, we were all hanging out near the bowling alley of our town, when a group of the seniors began, successfully, to persuade my teammate and classmate, who had been drinking on this occasion himself, to get a tattoo. Now I knew this guy's parents, and knew that they, like my own, would be so enraged if he got the tattoo that they would make him quit the basketball team. So I, in what I construed as the spirit of friendship—however adolescent—confronted my teammate with this challenge, that he would have to beat me up before he got the tattoo, because I wasn't going to let him do it. Now, at well over six feet tall, this boy would have had no trouble doing so. The issue was whether it was worth it to him to beat me up in order to get the tattoo. He considered it briefly, decided against it, and went on to play the season, tattoo-less. I thought that I had lived up to my duty as a friend.

In retrospect, this is obviously a silly, utterly adolescent incident. To make such a fuss about a tattoo, to see physical confrontation as the appropriate means of dissuasion, to even take the whole episode that seriously, clearly testifies to the immaturity of the participants, myself first of all. But there was also, it now seems to me, something important at work of which I had no cognizance at the time. Behind the adolescent immaturity was a conception of friendship at work which, however misguided in this instance, was the very one that I have been suggesting was the informing one of my youth: friendship as a demand relationship. I was not going to let my friend "do his own thing" by getting the tattoo that would lead, I was sure, to his basketball ruination. I was going to demand, or so I thought, that he do what was best, that he act so as to be the best that he could be. Silly in the specific details, the incident nevertheless was an exhibition of the very notion of friendship that has informed my experience ever since.

As I grew older, and especially in college, my friendships tended to be occasioned by the same circumstances. My teammates on the basketball team in college, as other essays have indicated, blessed me with a set of friendships close and deep. A number of things strike me about these friendships. First, as before, they were fundamentally demand relationships. As intensely competitive athletes, we expected the most of ourselves and each other. Part of the meaning of our friendship was that we always had to "live up" to the demands of that friendship, both on and off the court. In practices, we often played against each other, and the only way we would improve was if we challenged each other to be the best we could. In games, of course, we played together, yet still preserved the clear demand of each other to be the best we could. Though it may sound strange to those opposed ideologically to competition, there was no interesting difference in the character of our friendship between when we played with and when we played against each other. We were friends, and that meant that we challenged each other to excellence, always. Competition, no doubt, can bring about alienation. But to be true to my experience of things, I must avow that it can often be the source of the deepest of friendships.

Second, those friendships were not abstract in any way. They were occasioned, occasioned by an intense experience and an intense commitment in common—the commitment to having the best team we could. Part of the deep meaning, part of the depth, of those friendships, I'm now convinced, was a function of that shared commitment toward a common goal. We were all passionate, committed, competitive athletes, and the intensity of those individual commitments spilled over into our friendships, watering them with the same intensity and depth. During those years I learned that friendships do not arise *ex nihilo*. They are occasioned, occasioned by a shared commitment, and the deeper that shared commitment, the more deep the friendships are allowed to be. Nothing in my later experience has changed that conviction.

Third, however, that means that to an extent the passion of the friendship is also a function of the preservation of the passion of the shared commitment. After we graduated and went on to our separate careers, the passion of our friendships for each other, the peculiar intensity that characterized our relationships while teammates, surely diminished. We did not, as we at first naively expected, stay constantly in touch with each other and get together regularly. As our deep commitments shifted to other pursuits, so did our passionate friendships. Before long, we were seeing each other only rarely. I have read of similar experiences of those soldiers who are together in combat. Such incomparably intense experiences, not surprisingly, grow equally intense friendships. It is common, apparently, for such solders, upon discharge from the service, to swear eternal friendship, promise annual reunions, etc. Then, typically, such things never happen. The shared experience which occasioned the friendship is gone.

Does that mean that the friendships were ended, is it evidence that they were somehow superficial? I do not think so. There is an impossible demand sometimes put on friendships that they be somehow "eternal," independent of the circumstances in which they arise and which sustain them. Part of the concreteness of friendships is that they are occasioned, and the intensity of the friendship is in part a function of the intensity of the occasion. Without that intensity, it is impossible to expect the intensity of the friendship to continue in the abstract.

Moreover, my experience has been that those friendships do not literally end, even after the commitment which occasioned them is over. When I return occasionally to my college class reunions, I am often struck by the ease with which, after the briefest of conversations, my friendships with my former teammates are reaffirmed. In next to no time, we have reestablished the same rapport with each other, even if we have not seen each other for five or even ten years. To be sure, things are not as intense as they were when we were teammates. How could they be? It would be an impossible demand to lay upon our friendships that they retain that intensity interminably. The wonderful reaffirmation I experience at these reunions is enough, and it should be. In no sense is the reality or genuineness of our friendship diminished because the intensity is diminished by time and other commitments. We have to learn that friendships, too, as all human things, are temporal, defined, literally, by shared commitments and occasions.

Fourth, the "shared commitment" of which I have been speaking was not any old commitment. As brothers, and later, as teammates, Art and I were engaged in a shared commitment to excellence. To be sure, our specific concern, no doubt trivial in the larger scheme of things, was to becoming excellent basketball players. This should not be confused with nor reduced to the "desire to win." Our shared commitment was to being the best.

The way that being the best would be exhibited, to others and to ourselves, was to win lots of games. But winning, in this sense, is the "epiphenomenon," the immediate and finally superficial manifestation of the deeper commitment we shared and which occasioned our friendships: to be the best players we could be. In this sense, however naive, it was a version of the shared commitment to excellence, to *arete* in the Greek sense, that Aristotle argues is characteristic of the highest friendships. And, as I shall try to show presently, it rubbed off, in that my deepest friendships since those youthful athletic friendships have preserved the character of being demand relationships in a shared commitment to excellence, though the specific mode of that excellence came to be redefined by circumstances and life choices.

Later, as I established myself in my career as philosopher and teacher, I formed a number of close friendships with colleagues. These friendships, especially those that went beyond being simply the "casual" friendships that Aristotle calls friendships of utility or pleasure, shared many of the deeper characteristics of my earlier athletic friendships. They continued to be demand relationships, occasioned by a specific and shared commitment to excellence, by now the commitment to excellence in teaching or in philosophic insight. This convergence of elements is the best explanation I can offer for a phenomenon that has been true of my friendships and I know of many others as well. To wit, one does not form deep friendships either with people with whom one seems to disagree almost completely, nor with those (thankfully few) people with whom one agrees on virtually everything. In the former cases, the constant disagreement means that the element of shared commitment can never be established. These people often become our rivals, not our friends, and what is lacking that makes genuine friendship impossible, I suggest, is that crucial element of a *shared* commitment that, in my experience at least, is definitive of the deepest friendships. On the other hand, my experience on those few occasions when I meet someone who seems to agree with me on everything (usually students, and thankfully only for a short time, until they mature), is that the possibility of a deep friendship is inhibited by the lack of a genuine context in which the demand relationship can flourish. The lesson I learned from my athletic youth is reaffirmed in these situations: a genuine friend must be someone who, by occasionally standing *against* you in whatever the appropriate way, can issue the demand that you be the best you can be. That is why, I suppose, my deepest philosophic friendships have been with those people with whom I have a deep and abiding set of agreements, whether it be on philosophers in whom we are interested, ways of interpretation, or visions of excellence, yet at the same time who take standpoints sufficiently *different* from my own that we can issue to each other the demand to be our best which so informs my experience of friendship.

I raised in passing a moment ago the question of friendships with students. Three or four of the deepest, most sustained friendships with which I have been blessed have been with former students. Given what I have said so far, that should be neither surprising nor unusual. First of all, the teacher/student relationship is one whose very structure sets up the conditions I have described as characteristic of deep friendships: they are demand relationships, they are occasioned by our (initially happenstance) involvement in a shared commitment, and that shared commitment, in the best cases, is surely to excellence. Indeed, it is not difficult to see here some of the causes for the common *failure* of student/teacher relationships to attain to genuine friendship. The demand relationships may be entirely one-sided. The sense in which the teacher demands of the students is perhaps obvious (although one form of defective teaching is surely not to demand enough of one's students). But it is no less crucial that the students demand of the teacher and especially that the teacher *recognize* that the students also are demanding of him or her, that the teacher experience the reciprocity of that demand relationship. What the students are demanding, of course, is what the teacher is demanding of the students: excellence. Once again, if that shared commitment to excellence is lacking on either side, the student/teacher relationship will not fulfill its promise.

But when these factors converge, when the teacher and student become engaged in a mutual demand relationship founded in a shared commitment to the subject and to their being the best they can be, then the situation is ripe for genuine friendship, and it should not be surprising that I and others have found some of our deepest friendships arising out of this relationship. The gradual transition from student or teacher to friend is often so subtle as to be virtually unnoticed, and for good reason: the elements that the two relationships share make the transition, as we often say, "natural." My former students, now friends, share with me those crucial characteristics of a shared demand and a shared commitment to excellence. Like my basketball friendships, these too can be sustained at some distance in space and time.

Is there something "macho" about these experiences and the sense of friendship that I have developed out of them? Is what I have described a "guy thing"? Originating as they did in my involvement in athletics, including as they do the element of "competitive" demand relationships and goal-oriented striving, it might well be said that it is so. What of the so-called "feminine" traits of caring, or nurturing? Are they not incompatible with all this macho demanding, competing, and striving? I must speak to my experience rather than conceptual stereotypes and say that I have never found it so. Nurturing, after all means in part helping to grow, and I have found that one of the ways I have been "nurtured," aided in growing, is when the best was demanded of me by my friends, in whatever the context. Moreover and happily, many of these very friendships, particularly in my professional career and with my former students, have been with women. They seem to have entered into such demand relationships and such shared commitments to excellence with a passion and depth as strong as any man's. To be sure, my friendships with women are often complicated by the sense, absent in my male friendships, that there is a certain holding back from possibilities best not actualized. And I know, because they have told me, that the same is true for my homosexual friends in their non-sexual friendships with people of their own sex, including me. These friendships, to be sure, are complicated by the question of sexuality, sometimes in enjoyable, sometimes in frustrating ways. Complicated, but not necessarily diminished.

And what of love? To ask a very old question, can lovers be friends? We do not have to insist that love and friendship are identical to acknowledge how much they share. Love relationships, surely are demand relationships (in the failed cases often too much so), occasioned, always, by a set of complex shared commitments. Do they also involve a shared commitment to excellence? In the case of successful, sustained love relationships, my experience is that they do, that in myriad ways the two lovers are striving for excellence. Perhaps, indeed, one difference between our friendships and our loves is that the complex of shared commitments, and so of shared demands and strivings, is in our loves so much more varied, multiple. Is this not why we usually experience our friendships as "simpler" than our loves? Simpler, yes, but also similar, which is why so often the difference between them is so slight that we cannot say whether a given relationship is love or friendship. If we think first of their profound kinship, we might best say that it doesn't matter. What counts is the kinship.

Addendum

What strikes me first in retrospect is something I mentioned in passing in the earlier version: the possibility that my reflections on friendship will be taken by some readers as "macho," perhaps thus as "masculinist." Now, it is true enough that my early experiences of friendship occurred often in the then largely male context of competitive athletics. To say that, in my case at least, is simply to be honest. And what I have called the "demand relationship" character of my experience of friendship not only arose from that athletic context but, I would now want to avow, remains largely true to my experience even today. But with some significant modifications! As the range of my intense relationships expanded beyond the athletic context to friendships with colleagues, neighbors, and others whom I meet along the way, it strikes me that the element of "demand" has softened somewhat, perhaps become more complicated, but certainly not disappeared. I think now of friendship as entailing a *sharing* with my friends, a wanting to do what is best for them, what will make them happy. But sharing what? Aristotle remains right: often enough it is sharing pleasures, being useful to my friend in whatever way I can. But does it not remain the case that the pleasures I share I *want* to share because I think it will make their lives *better*? That doing what is best for them means doing what I think will make their lives better, and so more excellent? In that sense, I think that the element in friendship that I referred to perhaps too starkly as a "demand relationship" never really goes away. In the end, to want what is best for our friends means doing what we believe will make their lives better, more excellent. Today, I would surely no longer tell a friend that he or she would have to beat me up if they were thinking of getting a tattoo (one of my grandsons is now covering his body with them!). But if he or she were about to rob a bank, or do harm to someone, I might!

CHAPTER 7

Writing This

"The poet must have wide-angle vision
each look a world glance
and the concrete is most poetic."

LAWRENCE FERLINGHETTI

I WANT TO CLOSE these essays with a short reflection on the experience of writing them, for, so far as I can understand it, something happened in the writing of them that was rather different from what I had thought I was doing when I wrote the introduction some time ago. In that introduction I implicitly drew a distinction between two forms of philosophical writing, the one, the standard form of professional philosophic writing, in which one develops as clearly and persuasively as possible a given thesis, marshals as much evidence as one can in order to "prove" it, and perhaps considers and refutes alternative positions, and the other, which I thought I was going to try to do, to "evoke" matters for thought, use my experiences of this or that literally to "call forth" issues that I thought worthy of thoughtfulness. In that sense, borrowing the term from Mitchell Miller, I intended my essays to be "provocations" to thoughtfulness, to philosophy.

Perhaps they succeeded in doing that in some measure, and if so, that is all to the good. But as I reflect on what was happening as I wrote them, something else becomes thematic that could not be adequately captured by the notion of "evocation." In the term "evoking" a given issue or thought, I hear the literal sense of "calling it forth." But to "call it forth" carries with it the notion of bringing it to presence, having it before us in a way that we might "get hold" of it, even control or master it. In this sense, "evoking" an issue might be regarded as a propaedeutic to explaining it or proving it in the more orthodox philosophical sense. Having successfully evoked a previously hidden or perhaps opaque issue, it is now there, to be explained and analyzed philosophically. But I intended to do no such thing, and as far as I can see, have not done so.

I have come to think of these essays rather as exercises in what Martin Heidegger called "releasement" (*Gelassenheit*). Certainly from my vantage as writer, I was trying more to set these themes free, to *allow* them to be, to let them go. In these terms I hear the sense that I am no longer engaging in a quest for mastery, explanation, or proof, no longer even trying to bring the issue *before* my contemplative gaze, which is what evocation would do if successful. Letting them go means on the one hand getting them out because I as writer needed to get them out (in the words of the writer Joan Didion, we write in order to find out what we think), but also letting them go in the sense of releasing any claim to control over them, indeed, perhaps for a while, letting them gain control over me. Or perhaps not, for control is or should be no longer the issue. Freed, perhaps they would be allowed from time to time to "come over" the reader, as a certain mood might come over us, dwell with us for a while, and tincture our experience of things. They certainly came over me in that sense.

The sentiments of Joan Didion above ring true to me. Writing is *thinking*. We really do find out what we think by writing. One of the things I always tried to do with my students is to get them past the naïve view that in writing this or that paper, they are, in effect, functioning as the court stenographer for their brain, that in writing they are simply recording what they already know, writing down the already existing contents of their brains. Such an attitude makes writing get boring very fast. Better, again, to encourage them to think of writing as part of the process of thinking itself, indeed inseparable from it. Not something like "one must write what one has thought," but rather "one must write *in and as thinking.* Then writing might become *fun.*

I found trying to write in this way very, very challenging. Explaining, proving, refuting, the kind of writing I have done professionally throughout my career and the staple writing genre of professional philosophy, is, by contrast, far, far easier. If trying to write in the way I have here was difficult, trying to articulate its nature is even more so. Perhaps it is contradictory, trying to explain what precisely is not to be explained. I feel up against the limits of language here. Perhaps, at that limit, I should simply (simply!) release *it.*

As the Beatles have taught us, "Speaking words of wisdom, let it be."